ICELANDIC PATTERNS
in Needlepoint

JÓNA SPAREY

ICELANDIC PATTERNS
in Needlepoint

*Over 40 easy-to-stitch designs
from the Land of Ice and Fire*

Title page: Section from a tapestry by Angela McGill

*Dedicated to the original designers of the patterns
and to my Icelandic ancestors, who have
somehow instilled in my genes a love of Iceland
and its people's rich culture.*

Published by New Generation Publishing in 2018

ISBN: 978-1-78719-777-0

www.newgeneration-publishing.com

New Generation Publishing

CONTENTS

INTRODUCTION

In 1983 I held the first exhibition of my needlework at a North London gallery. The unusual designs, adapted from original Icelandic patterns aroused considerable interest and led to my teaching in this medium at colleges, art centres and also from home, which I hope has inspired and encouraged hundreds of students to produce many thousands of beautiful tapestries.

The aim of this book is to offer a wide selection of Icelandic needlepoint designs complete with charts, without concentrating on any one particular subject. It is first and foremost a *practical* book, so maximum space has been given to ideas and designs, rather than to beautifully designed photography showing the subject surrounded by decorative bits

and pieces. Instead, much of the layout of the book is dedicated to close-up colour photographs of sewn designs which are immediately followed by identical charts, each with symbols denoting colours, making it easy to check that you are using the correct colours by just flicking back the page.

Detailed instructions have also been given for sewing the designs from start to finish without using a frame, accompanied by helpful hints to achieve the perfect stitch. Having taught well over a thousand students over a nine-year period I find it quite easy to give written instructions in the same way as they are given verbally on my courses, which I hope will guide the stitcher step-by-step and stage-by-stage.

The colour schemes I have chosen for the various designs do not have to be copied exactly, but can be used as a guide in the choice of other colours – the emphasis today is often on matching colours to room decor.

Through my lectures and teaching I have come to realise how little people know about Iceland and its history (on my first day at school in Hertfordshire all my classmates were eagerly awaiting the arrival of an Eskimo!). For this reason there follows a brief history of Iceland and its people, which I hope will provide an interesting background to the needlepoint designs.

THE NORSE SETTLERS

The Norsemen settled in Iceland about 870. They travelled across the seas in longboats, bringing with them horses, cattle, dogs and sheep, of which the original breeds still exist today. The sheep were particularly hardy, having a very thick coat of wool which the settlers put to good use.

In 1783 the population of 83,000 experienced one of the worst volcanic eruptions in the history of the world, when over two hundred fissure volcanoes erupted, spewing out molten lava and, much worse, clouds of lava ash into the atmosphere. This then fell, covering the land, killing the animals, ruining the crops and causing a terrible famine. So violent was the eruption that clouds of lava ash were carried to Europe and even reached China! Only 42,000 of the population survived this disaster.

Nature, not content with this catastrophe, then produced a series of very severe winters, thus bestowing further hardships on the population. No wonder the Icelanders have such strong personalities! When people comment on mine, I simply answer: 'You haven't met my mother!'

Living in such a challenging country has produced a nation of independent and very determined people who have inherited a nationalistic pride in their past, their ancestors and their country.

This strength and independence is reflected in the embroidery of Iceland. My introduction to this rich world came when I was still a girl. My Icelandic mother, Svava, had settled in London in 1937 after marrying an Englishman, and in the school holidays I travelled to Iceland by trawler and was taught embroidery by my Icelandic grandmother, Hanna, in Reykjavik.

I was further inspired by the colourful embroideries displayed in the National Museum of Iceland. At that time no designs could be bought, but the residing Curator, Kristján Eldjárn, gave me many photographs of embroidery to copy. I also transcribed photographic transparencies onto graph paper, painstakingly reproducing the original designs.

Kristján Eldjárn's introduction to the book, *Ancient Icelandic Art* includes the following paragraph about Iceland's history of sewing:

> The feminine arts, needlework and weaving, were perhaps the most fertile branch of the arts practised in the past by the common people of Iceland in order to satisfy their creative needs and add beauty to their daily surroundings. To be skilled with one's hands has always been considered one of the finest attributes of woman, and it was a natural part of a young girl's schooling to study the feminine handicrafts with some skilled feminine artisan.

Today the population of Iceland is around 250,000, and it still amazes me how such a tiny nation can produce such a wealth of culture with their painters, sculptors, writers, poets, musicians and, of course embroiderers.

And yet, it is not all that surprising. To live in a land of such contrasting beauty is a unique experience. The island is only 300 miles (490km) east to

west and 195 miles (312km) north to south. It contains the largest glacier, waterfall and hot spring in Europe, and abounds in waterfalls, lakes and rivers, mountains, volcanoes and lava fields. It also plays host to thousands of nesting birds each summer.

Thanks to its position, Iceland has not been contaminated by the industrial air pollution of Europe. There are no factories to spoil the clarity of the crystal clean air – so marvellous for photography, as well as your lungs! Geothermal water is piped to most houses.

Iceland is a paradise for geologists, photographers, ornithologists, writers, artists and lovers of nature; it is easy to understand the pleasure and pride I feel when escorting visitors on one of my

'Grand Tours' of the island. They are always so captivated by this unique land of contrasts.

ICELANDIC EMBROIDERY

The National Museum in Reykjavik has a large collection of ecclesiastical and domestic embroideries. The oldest ecclesiastical pieces date back to the medieval period and include religious vestments, altar cloths and frontals, all lavishly decorated with embroidery.

Some domestic pieces date back to the fourteenth century. National costumes were always decorated with embroidery. The bottoms of the skirts were decorated with colourful flowers worked with crewel wool in split stitch, and the bodices were intricately sewn with leaves and flower patterns worked in silver or gold thread, using satin stitch. In addition, bed valances, coverlets, cushions and saddle cloths were all beautifully embroidered.

Housed in the Folklore Museum of Akureyri in the North of Iceland, is another very good collection of embroidery.

Perhaps one of the most interesting aspects of Icelandic embroidery is the close connection it has with the Bayeux Tapestry. The technique of laid couched work is very prominent, and is highly prized in Iceland. There are many fine examples of altar cloths sewn in this stitch, with four separate procedures required to produce the finished stitches.

Many women in the past, especially those in the highest ranks of society with more time to devote to embroidery, fulfilled the great demand for altar cloths, frontals and sacerdotal vestments.

Famous knights, bishops and scenes from the Bible were often depicted in Icelandic embroideries, and were surrounded by circular or polygonal frames. This method of framing dates back to the sixteenth-century Byzantine times. To enlarge the size of the work, geometric borders were added. These often depicted birds, animals, flowers and mythical beasts, but many borders were just simple geometric patterns, including twisted rope and knot designs. Repeating patterns were also used, and you will find examples of all these designs adapted for the needlepoint projects in this book.

The National Museum of Iceland also holds seventeenth- and eighteenth-century pattern books which were used by housewives for design ideas for knitting, weaving and embroidery. The patterns were derived from various sources, including Europe. These were collected together in just the same way as today we save our favourite cookery recipes and keep them in a book or folder.

Wool was used extensively for a variety of items such as horsecloths, and for clothing, which included shawls, socks, skirts, hats and mittens. The wool was woven, knitted, crocheted or embroidered depending on its usage. The colour of the sheep's wool varied in shades from black through to white, with delicate shades of pinky browns in between, and these natural colours were used to highlight the geometric patterns. The wool that was spun and then knitted is called Lopi wool. It is extremely warm and soft, but hairy. I am reminded of my time as a child in London; when the first cold weeks of autumn arrived mother insisted that my two sisters and I wore woolly vests that grandmother in Iceland had knitted for us. How they made us itch – we itched for a week, and the nuns at our convent school must have thought we had something more than just woolly vests!

Natural dyes were found in blueberries, moss and lichen, and it was mostly these dyes that were used for embroidery wools. Fine dyed crewel wool was worked on linen, while thicker strands of wool were used on tabby woven woollen cloth. Designs were sometimes carved onto wooden blocks which were then dipped into powdered chalk and stamped onto the dark woven cloth, leaving a pattern ready to embroider.

THE ICELANDIC TAPESTRY SCHOOL

Although my school is called The Icelandic Tapestry School, it should be made clear that the word tapestry actually means woven work, as worked on a loom. Usually my work is described as hand tapestry or needlepoint, which is generally worked in cross stitch on canvas, as opposed to embroidery which conjures up ideas of fancy stitches such as satin, stem and chain stitch.

Perhaps the most intriguing aspect of Icelandic embroidery is that the embroiderers work without the use of a cumbersome frame, even for larger pieces of work. There is no record of a frame having ever been used in Iceland. The work stays absolutely square due to the double-stranded canvas, the

This treasured family portrait shows Jón (Zöega), my grandfather and Hanna, my grandmother with their children: Uncle Venni (centre), Auntie Nanna (front) and my mother

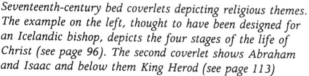

Seventeenth-century bed coverlets depicting religious themes. The example on the left, thought to have been designed for an Icelandic bishop, depicts the four stages of the life of Christ (see page 96). The second coverlet shows Abraham and Isaac and below them King Herod (see page 113)

stitch and the method of holding the canvas. This enables the needleworker to work twice as fast and for the tapestry to be completely portable. Many of my students take their tapestries on holiday, working away the hours on long flights. Those who are unfortunate enough to become ill or suffer from depression, or who have recently suffered a bereavement, find that needlepoint becomes a therapeutic pastime, completely absorbing their mind and letting them lose themselves in the sewing.

My students always work from charts, sewing directly onto the virgin canvas. This is much easier than one might think: after all, most people can count! One experiences great satisfaction when working from a chart rather than onto a printed canvas, which might be likened to painting by numbers. Besides, some printed canvases are not very accurate because the colours have been off-set

when printed, making it difficult for the stitcher to decide exactly where a certain colour is to go. Charts, on the other hand, have symbols denoting different colours, so there is never any hesitation about which colour should be used for each stitch. Once my students have learned how easy it is to work from a chart they never go back to printed canvases – surely an indication of how satisfying it is to work from a chart.

The canvas used by the Icelandic Tapestry School is an unusual 'count', having nine stitches to the inch (2.5cm). It is double stranded and is exclusively imported for me from Germany. Furthermore, it is easy to see and perfectly suited to Appleton tapestry wools – although many other threads and materials would also be suitable for these designs.

Most of the patterns I use are geometric, which gives them a strong character, and many people find them refreshingly different from the usual designs found in our shops today. They have certainly attracted a great deal of interest here in Britain since I began to run courses and give lectures, and introduced designs produced in kit form.

TECHNIQUES

Under this section we will tackle the art of stitching without a frame and attaining perfect tension, as well as the actual setting of the stitches.

STITCHING WITHOUT A FRAME

Always use double-stranded canvas, preferably antique in colour, as white can sometimes show through the wool. The double strands help to keep your work square, unlike single canvas, which should always be worked on a frame.

An unusual 'nine count' (a convenient way of expressing the more usual 'nine stitches to the inch') canvas is used at the Icelandic Tapestry School. This is perfect for working full cross stitch in Appleton wools. Being slightly larger mesh than the more usual ten stitches to the inch makes it easier to see and count. Readers requiring this canvas should write to the Icelandic Tapestry School for a price list. It is quite possible to use ten stitches to the inch canvas, but it is quite a struggle to pull the wool through when working in full cross stitch.

The rougher or raised side of the canvas is the correct surface to work on, as this side raises your stitch slightly. Do not worry too much if you cannot identify the correct surface, but if you do, mark it with a cross.

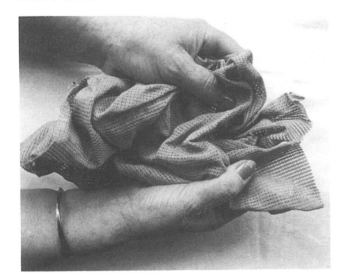

Fig 1

Working without a frame the canvas is held in a particular way, and must be softened by crumpling in your hands (see Fig 1). When the finished tapestry is pressed the canvas will regain its original stiffness.

If you have already tried to work without using a frame you may be familiar with the diamond shape that your work ends up, and with the problems of stretching it square again (see Fig 2). There are, however, ways to avoid this.

Many people are familiar with half cross stitch and tent stitch, but in my opinion neither of these is hard wearing enough; tent stitch, especially, when the thickness of the wool is actually underneath the work, loses the benefit of being hard wearing. Both these stitches go in one direction only, and without a frame can produce a very 'skew-whiff' tapestry.

Fig 2

HOLDING THE CANVAS

The area to be worked is stretched over the first two fingers, the canvas clamped between the thumb and third finger (see Fig 3 overleaf). The working area must always be stretched and held square, not on a slant. Working in this way will guarantee that the finished tapestry will be absolutely square.

This method of holding may feel awkward at first as you are using muscles in your hands not usually exercised in this way, but in time you will find it easier and will notice that your hands get stronger. This strengthening of the hand is particularly good for people who suffer from arthritis or rheumatism; these students often notice an improvement in their hands. If you are left-handed you should find no trouble working in the same manner, but please, stitch with your *left* hand. One of my students worked right-handed through a two-day course even though she was actually left-handed, because I had said that she should work exactly as I did!

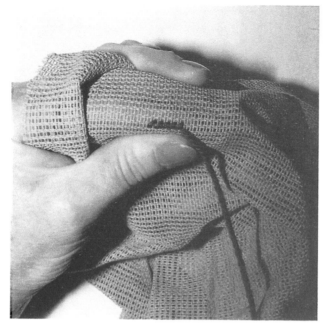

Fig 3

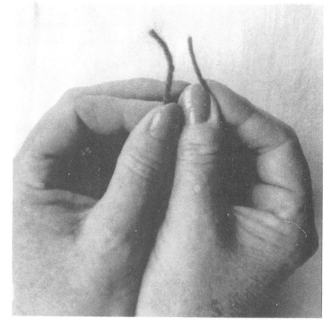

Fig 4

START AT THE CENTRE

Start your pattern at the centre of the canvas, working in small areas of colour and gradually radiating out to the sides as well as upwards and downwards, so stretching the canvas to the edges. This helps to keep the work flat and square. Never turn your canvas, as your stitches will be going in different directions. Mark the top edge with a piece of red wool to remind you. Use each shape as a stepping stone to reach the next part of the pattern.

When you have completed the pattern, then work the background. Start by filling in all the 'trapped' areas in the centre, working upwards and downwards from the centre once again.

STITCHING STEP-BY-STEP

Having softened your canvas, and learnt how to hold it, proceed to the wool and needle stage. Before threading the wool check that the length is no more than 46cm (18in) long. Then compare the ends. If one end is thicker, thread the needle with this end to avoid thick, clod-hopping stitches (see Fig 4).

FULL CROSS STITCH

Remember that the horizontal strands on your canvas represent your *row* and the vertical strands represent your *stitches*. Do not count the holes as stitches. Fig 5 shows exactly where the stitch is formed, and precisely where the horizontal and

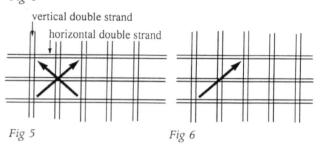

Fig 5   Fig 6

vertical lines cross each other. The holes are only there for the needle to go in. Always sew from bottom to top over the horizontal strand (see Fig 6).

Do not knot the wool when you begin to sew; instead hold 2.5cm (1in) of wool underneath the canvas, catching some of the wool with the needle as you stitch (see Fig 7). Always start in this way for it holds the wool securely.

Fig 7

Always work your row left to right (see Fig 8), then come back on the line to cross your stitches right to left (see Fig 9).

The needle is placed in and out of the canvas or material in one action. Try to remember that the needle always, always, always comes out vertical

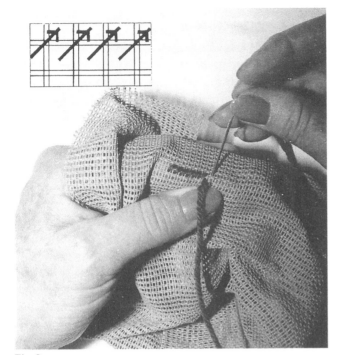

Fig 8

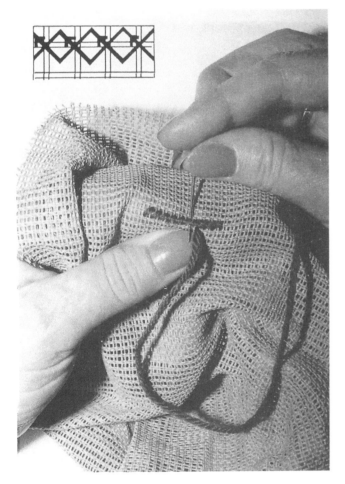

Fig 9

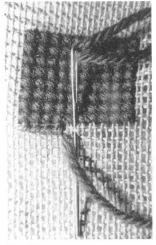

Fig 10

Fig 11

and straight, coming out of the hole immediately below where it went in (see Fig 10).

Now sew ten full cross stitches in a row onto your canvas and ten rows down (see Fig 11).

FINISHING OFF

Always try to complete a row of stitches before finishing off your wool; at the very least, complete the row one way. Finish off by running your needle through the back of five stitches on the previous row, not the row you have just completed (see Fig 12). Do not try to run the needle through the whole stitch at the back because this could distort your row. Instead, just pick up a few strands of each stitch, then cut the wool off flush with the canvas.

Fig 12

TWIDDLE YOUR NEEDLE!

As you proceed with your work have you noticed your thread twisting? This is because you stitch in and out of the canvas in one movement, the wool having a natural tendency to twist. To counteract this spiralling you must twiddle your needle half a turn anti-clockwise towards the palm of your hand. This action is best done as you pull the wool out and the needle is at its highest point before coming down again to do the next stitch (see Fig 13 overleaf).

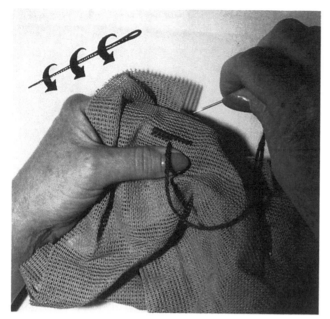

Fig 13

Practise, and check that with each stitch the relaxed wool looks the same as in Fig 14 – in the shape of a 'U'. In time this will become an instinctive action.

Fig 14

Great importance should be given to this action, for if the wool is allowed to stay twisted the action of pulling a double twisted thickness of wool through the hard canvas will wear it to a scraggy strand, giving a scraggy stitch. Were you in one of my classes you could not get away with sewing with

a twisted thread, because on inspection of your work the actual stitches would show the ugly twist. My students refer to me as 'eagle eye' and they often hear my voice ring out with, 'Twiddle your needle, twiddle your needle'. (By the way, the students also call me 'elephant ears'!!)

Try not to 'saw' your wool along the hard canvas as this will wear away the soft wool in no time. If the wool for any reason does become thin, finish off and use a new piece. Do not forget to thread the thickest end of the strand of wool into the needle.

TENSION

Look carefully at the stitch you are sewing. You will see it flatten down on the canvas as you gradually pull the wool up towards your shoulder. Now pull the wool very firmly until the stitch will not move any more – *this* is the perfect tension. When coming back to cross your stitch – right to left – pull the wool and needle towards your left shoulder, this helps the stitch to lie down neatly (see Fig 15).

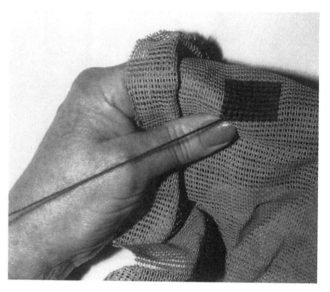

Fig 15

You may have noticed that the thickness of the wool can vary from colour to colour. This is due to the amount of alum that has been used in the water to fix the dye into the wool. More alum is required for strong and dark colours, less for pastel colours. The latter retain their woolly fluffiness, staying extremely soft, and therefore wearing away quickly if badly sewn, whilst the darker colours are less fluffy but much stronger. You must adjust the tension accordingly where you have dark and light colours together.

In some cases it is better to sew the lighter section of the work first, followed by the darker area of stitches. The fluffy lighter colour can spread over onto the darker stitches if they are put in first.

It is impossible to keep the wool from wearing to some degree as it is pulled through the canvas. When nearing the end of a length of wool it will be at its thinnest, and the tension should be slackened off accordingly.

Conversely, be very firm in your tension at the start of a new piece of wool, when it is at its thickest.

I have heard students remark that perhaps they should leave the very light colours until last, in case they get dirty. Clean hands are usually the answer to this. Some people, though, do have a rather acidic sweat and find that their needles tend to last only a week before they go black because the chrome is literally being eaten away by the acid. The film of chrome allows the needle to slide easily through the canvas and when the needle becomes black it is quite difficult to pull it through.

It is helpful to dust your hands with a little talc, and possibly you will need to change your needle more often. So keep an eye on your needle – and now, at least, you will understand what has happened to it.

PRESSING THE FINISHED WORK

When you have completed your design, check carefully for any missed stitches or for any stitches that have not been fully crossed.

Place the work face down on a clean bedsheet and, using a damp cloth, press the back of the tapestry with a hot iron. The wool will absorb some of the water. Turn the work face up and measure the tapestry horizontally across the top, across the middle, and across the bottom. If the tapestry is uneven, tease the canvas to an even size by pulling at it gently. When the work is square, press once again face down. Allow to dry on a flat surface for twenty-four hours.

START WITH A SAMPLER

It is very tempting as a beginner, to start stitching a lovely tapestry without reading the 'small print'. Any beginners reading this, please first make a small sampler, on which you can practise and even make mistakes. Having made a mistake, do not unpick the stitches, but leave them in as a reminder not to do it again.

Making a sampler is the best way of introducing the beginner to the method of holding the canvas, achieving the perfect tension for each stitch, and picking up all the little gems of wisdom which one day will culminate in the perfect tapestry.

At the beginning of a course my students sometimes apologise for being completely ignorant of the subject, but these are often the easiest people to teach, as they have no bad habits to break.

Some students get themselves in a panic, worrying too much about what they are supposed to be doing. Reading pages of written instructions can be very confusing. The following steps, in short paragraphs along with diagrams, should be easier to follow.

The best size for a beginner's sampler is 36 × 36cm (14 × 14in). If you are going to work on nine-count canvas you will have nine stitches to the inch (2.5cm), giving a total of 126 stitches square. Allow 13 stitches for a hem or turning all round. You will then be left with 100 stitches square. (Nine-count canvas is available in various sizes from the Icelandic Tapestry School.)

It is a good idea to work out the lay-out of your design roughly before starting your sampler. What do you want it to include? Names or initials, pet dog or cat, car, horse, dates, house, baby, piano, or butterfly . . . ?

The photographs show samplers worked by some of my students and you may notice that they all have something in common – a number of plain squares of stitches. These are the very first stitches to be made on the sampler. So begin by completing a few squares of full cross stitch to practise holding the canvas without the use of a frame.

On the next few pages you will find charted a selection of patterns to choose for your sampler. They have been placed roughly in categories, eg alphabet and numbers, animals, children and so on. So to personalise your own sampler, you can include your or someone else's name or initials, dates to commemorate an event, such as the birth of a new baby, or Christmas items (if you happen to be stitching at that time of the year). Perhaps you would like to record a sport or pastime or maybe an anniversary. Always remember to date your sampler – many of them will survive for perhaps hundreds of years.

DESIGNING THE LAYOUT

This is not strictly necessary, but some people like to organise their sampler in some way. Many of my students have begun with plain squares of stitches and gone on from there.

To design the layout of your sampler, proceed as follows. Having decided on your designs copy them out onto graph paper (preferably 5mm size, which is obtainable from most stationers in an A4 pad – I find my students are often given the wrong size, so insist). It is a good exercise to copy out designs onto graph paper, as it helps you to understand how the design is formed and you will make fewer mistakes when actually stitching.

Now cut out each design and arrange them on a card or a piece of paper, moving them about until you are satisfied with their positions. Take another look at the students' samplers for ideas.

ABC, 123 ▶
Where possible, try to use a medium to dark shade of wool for lettering and numbers

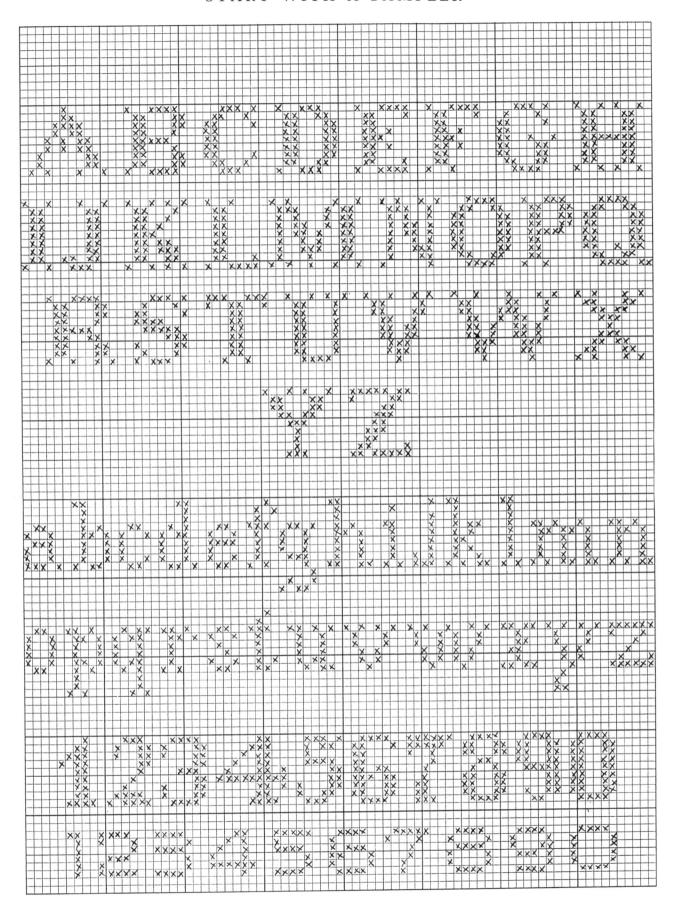

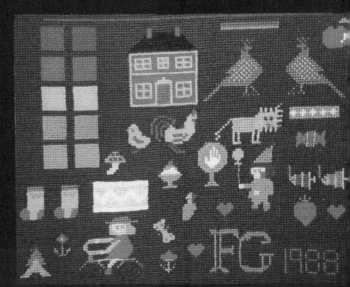

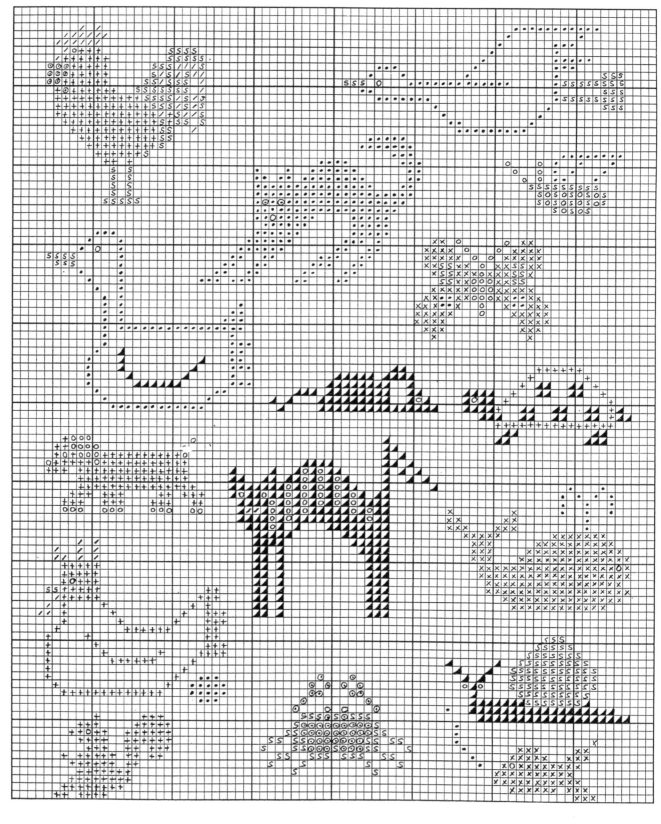

SAMPLER PATTERNS

X Blue	◢ Grey	/ Pink or Red	V Green	• White or Beige
○ Black	+ Brown	S Yellow	⊙ Orange	

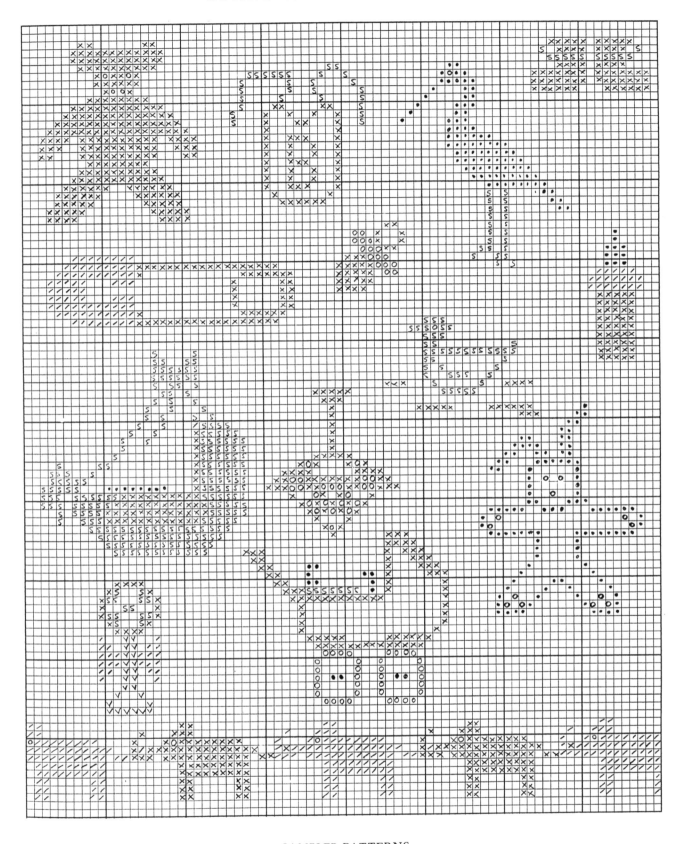

SAMPLER PATTERNS

X Blue   ○ Black   / Pink or Red   V Green   ● White or Beige   S Yellow

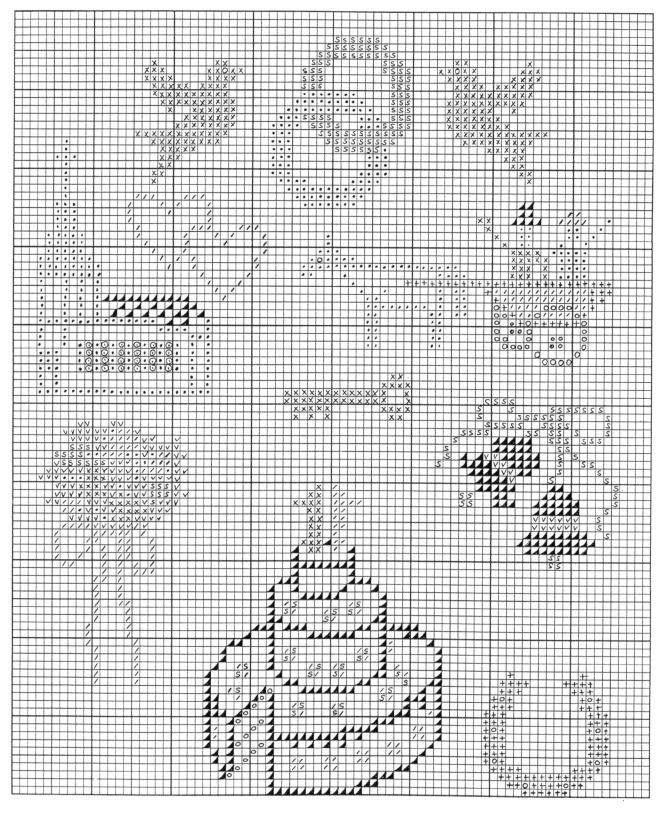

SAMPLER PATTERNS

X Blue ◢ Grey / Pink or Red V Green • White or Beige

○ Black + Brown S Yellow ⊙ Orange

SAMPLER PATTERNS

X Blue	◢ Grey	/ Pink or Red	V Green	● White or Beige
○ Black	+ Brown	S Yellow	☉ Orange	

OLIVE AND WALTER'S SAMPLER

Having completed your beginner's sampler you might feel ambitious enough to tackle a sampler for a special occasion, such as the one shown below.

This sampler was made to commemorate forty years of marriage between Olive and Walter, who also celebrated by accompanying me on one of my grand tours of Iceland. Olive was one of my students for many years. One day she asked if I could draw a Lancaster Bomber – that was the beginning of her sampler.

As Olive and Walter are both Londoners the top heading had to be the Houses of Parliament. St

Paul's Cathedral is depicted because of their involvement in the church. Walter had spent three years as a Radio Operator in the Royal Air Force, hence the Lancaster Bomber and RAF badge. The LNER steam engine is in memory of Olive's grandfather, father and uncles, all employees of LNER.

Walter's fifty years as a church organist is shown by the church organ – the pipes are sewn in gold thread to give the impression of metal. A few tools remind us of Walter's DIY enthusiasm, while the microscope is also sewn in gold thread (to suggest its brass element) reflecting a career in pathology.

The burning house reminds them of the war years together, and illuminated manuscripts show Olive's

interest in them during her career as a librarian. Olive is also a pianist so a grand piano, with notes, had to be included, as well as pots of flowering plants and garden wellies showing her interest in gardening.

The birth signs for each partner have been included, and the couple are seen holding hands. A cat sits between them under a bower of roses, with the Sussex Downs and the sea in the background. Their daughter's name, Ann, is stitched at the top with her husband's name, Terry, at the bottom, with their children's names, Christopher and Caroline, on each side.

CHILD'S SAMPLER

This is a particularly colourful child's sampler from the National Museum in Reykjavik. The young girl, Vilborg Gunnarsdottir, has stitched the designs in full cross stitch.

Incidentally, there are no actual surnames in Iceland such as Mrs Smith, or Mr Brown. All children inherit, as their surname, their father's Christian name with son or daughter added on the end. Think of your father's Christian name and, depending whether you are male or female, put son or daughter at the end of it.

My father was English and was called Eric. Had he been Icelandic my name would have been Jóna Ericsdottir – Jóna, daughter of Eric. Then someone would say, 'I know two Erics in that village, which one was he?' I would reply, 'Eric Georgesson.' 'Oh, Eric, son of George, I know who you mean'! Now we can understand where the surname Johnson originated.

Better still, a lady never loses her identity when she gets married – she keeps her own name and is then known as the wife of, say, Eric Georgesson.

BORDERS

There are various methods for framing your design with a border. Perhaps the easiest is to place one border at the top and bottom, and a different border at each side. The two ways of doing this are shown in Figs 1 and 2.

Fig 1

Fig 2

Fig 3

Fig 4

Fig 5

If you want the same border to go all the way around your design, a rather more complicated process needs to be followed. A straightforward method is detailed below.

First, find the middle of each of the four sides of your design (see Fig 3). Then decide which section of your border is going to marry up to the middle of the sides of your design: examples are shown in Figs 4 and 5.

Begin stitching your border at the centre, working outwards to the left-hand side and then to the right-hand side for the top and bottom borders, and up and down for the side borders. Never turn your canvas around, as then your stitches would be going in different directions. Square each border off at the corners (see Fig 6).

28

Fig 6

Fig 8

The space you are left with at each corner can be tackled in different ways. You could count how many stitches there are horizontally and vertically in your space, then draw the exact size onto some graph paper and make up a little design for this space to complement your border design (see Fig 7).

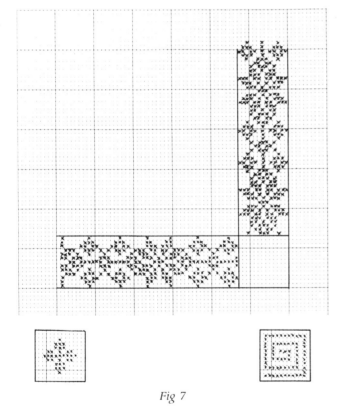

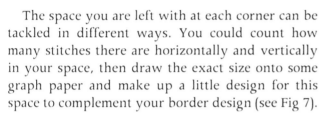

Fig 7

Alternatively, you could use the four corner spaces as an opportunity to insert your initials and date (see Fig 8). It is nice to incorporate your initials and the date into all stitched work, as the finished pieces are

often handed down through generations, making an interesting family heirloom.

It is possible to join the borders together at the corners by photocopying your border design a few times, then cutting the copies out with scissors. If you then marry up your cut-out border to your actual border, the ends can be mitred and the two sections joined together, resulting in a design for the corner space (see Fig 9). This is, of course, a trial-and-error technique and does not always produce a satisfactory design.

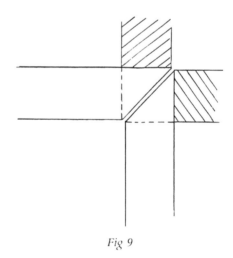

Fig 9

BORDERS (pages 30–7)

All the borders shown on these pages are worked in Appleton tapestry wool on nine-count, double stranded canvas, with a size 20 tapestry needle.

Quantities of wool given are for the length of border shown in the photograph.

1	APPLETON NO/COLOUR	SKEINS
/	981 Beige	6
=	159 Dk Green	1
S	155 Med Green	1
•	152 Lt Green	1
X	757 Deep Pink	2
O	755 Pale Pink	1
⊙	205 Salmon	1
‖	714 Dull Mauve	1
V	607 Purple	1

2	APPLETON NO/COLOUR	SKEINS
•	641 Lt Green	3
+	159 Dk Green	1
O	643 Med Green	1
⊙	948 Dk Pink	2
⊙	944 Med Pink	1
/	941 Baby Pink	1
S	758 Maroon	1

3	APPLETON NO/COLOUR	SKEINS
/	981 Beige	6
S	749 Midnight Blue	1
•	746 Med Blue	1
O	461 Pale Blue	1
⊙	716 Wine Red	1
+	713 Dirty Pink	1
X	157 Turquoise	1

1

2

3

4

1		APPLETON NO/COLOUR	SKEINS
/		693 Yellow	4
||		861 Salmon	1
=		604 Med Lilac	1
•/		602 Lt Lilac	1
O		607 Dk Lilac	1
S		141 Pale Pink	1
X		316 Dk Olive	1
•		313 Gld Olive	1

2		APPLETON NO/COLOUR	SKEINS
X		992 Off White	4
O		716 Wine Red	2
S		757 Deep Pink	1
•/		755 Med Pink	1
||		754 Pink	1
•		752 Palest Pink	1

3		APPLETON NO/COLOUR	SKEINS
/		747 Midnight Blue	4
X		741 Pale Blue	1
X		745 Med Blue	1
O		885 Pale Lilac	1
S		103 Med Lilac	1

4		APPLETON NO/COLOUR	SKEINS
X		692 Yellow	4
S		716 Wine Red	1
||		805 Cerise	1
O		144 Deep Pink	1
•		942 Pale Pink	1
=		348 Dk Green	1
/		344 Lt Green	1

1

	APPLETON NO/COLOUR	SKEINS
/	935 Plum Brown	4
•	157 Dk Turquoise	1
+	154 Lt Turquoise	1
II	974 Grey Green	1
X	505 Dk Russet	1
O	205 Lt Russet	1
S	607 Dk Purple	1
V	601 Very Lt Mauve	1

2

	APPLETON NO/COLOUR	SKEINS
+	991 White	4
O	148 Xmas Red	1
V	833 Xmas Green	1
•	694 Yellow	1
S	Gold	1

3

	APPLETON NO/COLOUR	SKEINS
/	529 Green	4
O	866 Dk Orange	2
V	862 Lt Orange	1
X	473 Yellow	1
S	Gold	1

4

	APPLETON NO/COLOUR	SKEINS
+	157 Dk Turquoise	4
•	585 Brown	2
X	693 Yellow	2
S	623 Orange	1

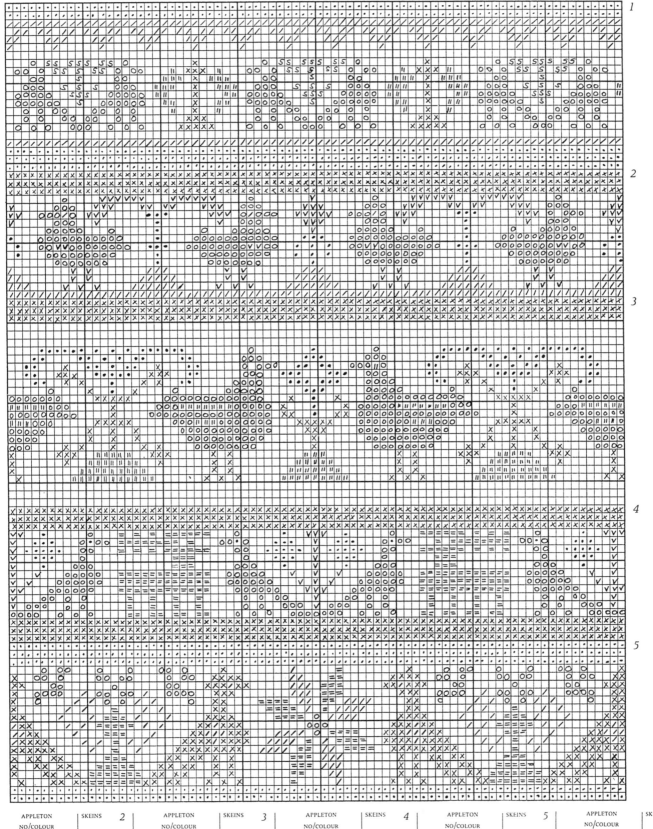

1	APPLETON NO/COLOUR	SKEINS	2	APPLETON NO/COLOUR	SKEINS	3	APPLETON NO/COLOUR	SKEINS	4	APPLETON NO/COLOUR	SKEINS	5	APPLETON NO/COLOUR	SKEINS
•	962 Grey	3	X	121 Pinky Beige	3	□	529 Dk Turquoise	4	X	984 Beige	3	•	883 Lt Grey	4
/	529 Dk Turquoise	1	O	472 Yellow	2	O	993 Black	2	V	347 Olive Green	1	O	562 Lt Blue	1
X	528 Med Turquoise	1	V	124 Lt Brown	1	•	861 Lt Orange	1	=	976 Elephant Grey	1	=	747 Dk Blue	1
‖	525 Lt Turquoise	1	•	128 Med Brown	1	X	623 Med Orange	1	O	716 Dk Wine	1	/	525 Med Turquoise	1
O	567 Dk Blue	1	/	585 Dk Brown	1	‖	865 Dk Orange	1	•	472 Yellow	1	X	529 Dk Turquoise	1
S	564 Lt Blue	1												

THE DESIGNS

The needlepoint designs in this book can be used – and adapted – in a multitude of ways: as wall hangings, stool and chair seats, bell pulls, table runners, samplers and cushions. They are also interchangeable so that, for instance, some framed picture designs can become cushions and vice versa.

MATERIALS

In the lists which follow, quantities of wool required to reproduce the designs as photographed are given to the nearest skein, but everyone stitches with a different tension. By working tightly less wool is used, while loosely sewn work uses considerably more. The wool quantities given are generous.

All charts are worked in Appleton wools, with the exception of Grandmother's Cushion, page 78. For this design, a single strand of Paterna wool is used.

All other charts are worked in Appleton *tapestry* wools, except two small repeating patterns (page 46) which are worked in Appleton *crewel* wools, using only one strand, worked on fourteen-count double-stranded canvas, antique colour, not white.

All designs are worked on nine-count double-stranded canvas (available from the Icelandic Tapestry School), apart from the three exceptions mentioned above. Grandmother's Cushion is worked on floba fabric, which has eighteen strands to the inch. Work over two strands giving nine stitches to the inch.

Floba and fourteen-count canvas are both available from the Icelandic Tapestry School.

COLOUR KEYS

Different symbols on the charts denote different colours. The symbols for each design have been entered in the column alongside the Appleton wool reference numbers with a brief description of each colour, eg, S.202 light beige. Quantities of wool for nine-count canvas for each design are given with the keys.

Appleton wools are stocked by many good needlecraft shops. If you have difficulties, a price list is available from the Icelandic Tapestry School for wools and canvas for each design.

WALL HANGINGS AND FRAMED PICTURES

Never put glass over a wool tapestry, as wool is a natural fibre and needs to breathe. The work just requires a gentle brush down now and then.

Some years ago a student covered her work with glass, hanging her masterpiece on a wall which, unbeknown to her, was very damp. The whole work became covered in mildew. However, woollen tapestries with no glass *can* be hung in the bathroom – the steam does them no harm at all.

Cotton and silk work does need more protection and generally should be covered by glass.

FRAMING

Framing is a skill which you may have mastered; however, it is probably wiser in most cases to use a professional picture framer for your completed embroidery. Always shop around first as prices vary enormously. Remember to tell them that you do not want glass. Some framers may try to argue the point, but stand firm and tell them – Jóna said *no glass*!

Alternatively, you can stretch your tapestry over a piece of blockboard (*not* cardboard) cut to size, stretching and fixing your work by stapling the canvas down at the back (see Fig 1). The edge can either be left with the canvas showing, or can be

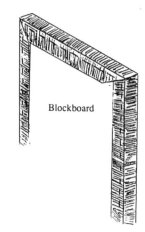

Blockboard

Fig 1

covered with strips of veneer, tacked down with small brass pins.

The design for the round Foxglove Cushion (see page 86) is ideal as a wall hanging, and because round frames are difficult to come by and very expensive, the blockboard method can be applied. A carpenter or someone with a 'router' will need to cut the round piece of blockboard.

Do not hang your masterpiece over your cooker, nor over the chair of a habitual pipe or cigarette smoker. Grease and nicotine will not enhance your work at all. Instead, find a suitable location – preferably not in direct sunlight – and, do not forget the bathroom!

ICELANDIC CUSHIONS

Most Scandinavian homes contain lovely cushions, many sewn in cross stitch with luxuriously ruched velvet or satin surrounds. Iceland is no exception. The cushions hold a very special place in the decor of Icelandic homes, as this little story shows.

My Auntie Sigga had invited my group to her home for a buffet luncheon. Before the members of the group arrived my aunt began to pack away some of her beautiful cushions. I explained that my group was usually well behaved, and did not scatter food about, but she laughed and said, 'Don't be so silly, child, I am packing away my everyday cushions; go to the hall cupboard and take out the best ones.'

My mother gave me some of my grandmother's cushions, and to find out how the ruching was done the cushion surround had literally to be taken apart. The designs I supply from the Icelandic Tapestry School have the surround as an optional extra, completed and sewn ready for you to slip-stitch in your tapestry. Some of my students were not over-impressed at first sight of them, but eventually agreed that they did seem to grow on you, and gave a final touch of luxury to the design.

The following instructions will help you make up your own ruched velvet surrounds for appropriate designs in this book.

♦ Use the lightest weight velvet you can find, such as a rayon velvet (used more often for dress-making than upholstery).
♦ Use machine stitching where possible, although the velvets can be sewn by hand.
♦ Use nylon thread – 40 weight.
♦ Use large stitches – approx ½cm (¼in).
♦ Use a loose tension.
♦ Leave long pieces of thread at the beginning *and* end of the rows, to be gathered for the ruching – approx 15.5cm (6in).
♦ Use feather-filled cushion pads where possible.

Instructions are given for making up two ruched velvet surrounds, one square and one circular. Measurements for fabric required for all the other cushions are given; use the examples shown here as a guide for making up the other velvet surrounds.

AUTUMN PAIR OF CUSHIONS: SQUARE RUCHED SURROUND

The instructions given are for the designs on pages 74 and 75, but can be easily adapted for other cushion sizes. Layout is shown in Fig 2.

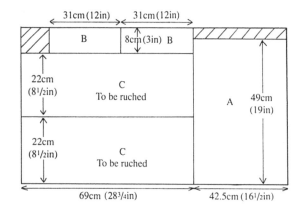

Fig 2

The piece of velvet should be 52 × 122cm (20½ × 48in), consisting of:
Back panel 49 × 42.5cm (19 × 16½in)
Two panels for top and bottom sections 31 × 8cm (12 × 3in)
Two panels for sides to be ruched 22 × 69cm (8½ × 27in) each

TO MEASURE AND CUT OUT PANELS
Measure and mark material into panels with tailor's chalk to size as specified above.

Alternatively, make patterns in paper of above sizes and pin to material, chalking a line around each one. Remove paper patterns and cut out.

TO ASSEMBLE
Take top and bottom panels (B) and turn under 2cm (¾in) on one edge of each; stitch down close to fold.

This stitched edge will eventually be sewn to the tapestry (see Fig 3). Now leave to one side.

Next take the two side panels (the ruching pieces – C). Place on the table right side up and turn over 5.5cm (2in) (see Fig 4).

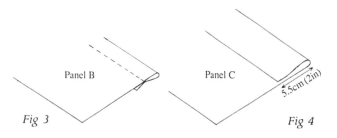

Fig 3   Fig 4

Machine stitch 2cm (³⁄₄in) in at each end from the fold to within 1cm (³⁄₈in) from the edge (see Fig 5).

Turn the fold right side out. Snip on left side hem close to stitches. Now stitch 3.5cm (1¼in) in from the folded edge, leaving 15.5cm (6in) of thread either end (see Fig 6).

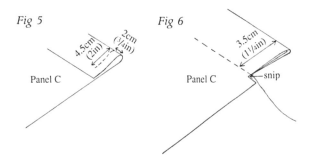

Fig 5   Fig 6

Take the other edge of the panel and fold under 2cm (³⁄₄in). Stitch down close to fold using loose tension. (This edge will eventually be sewn to the tapestry.)

Fold the velvet left between the two rows of stitches on panels C in half, and make a 0.5cm (¼in) pleat on the fold (see Fig 7).

You should now have three lots of threads 15.5cm (6in) long on either side again (see Fig 7).

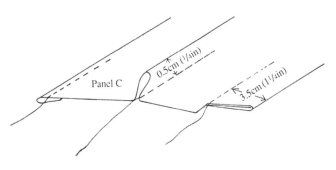

Fig 7

Now gently pull up all three rows of stitching, carefully gathering in the velvet by hand until it measures 43.5cm (17in) (see Fig 8). Fasten off securely by hand stitching in back stitch several times.

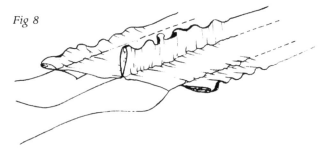

Fig 8

The next step is to lay the two ruched panels onto the two flat panels right side up, overlapping them by 2cm (³⁄₄in) (see Fig 9).

Machine over the line of gathered stitches on the two ruched panels, right side up. The front section of the surround is now complete.

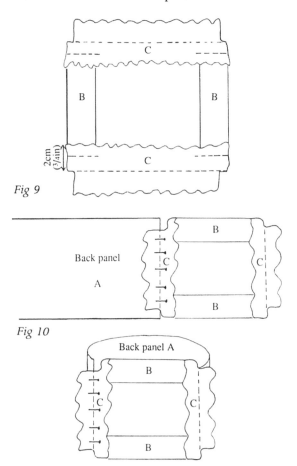

Fig 9

Fig 10

Place this completed section right side up, slide the back panel (also right side up) 5.5cm (2in) under the completed front section (see Fig 10).

Tack or pin together along the line of gathered stitches, then machine stitch securely.

Fold back panel under front, turning other side edge in by 2cm (³/₄in). Again tack or pin to front section and machine down on top (right side up) along line of gathered stitches. Turn inside out and tack together the two open side seams by 2cm (³/₄in).

Your surround is now complete. Turn the right way up and insert your selected cushion or filling. Hand sew your tapestry in a blind hemming stitch to the velvet casement.

Experienced sewers should have no problem with the assembly of these velvet casements, but if you feel it is too complicated they are available from the Icelandic Tapestry School already assembled.

SMALL ROUND CUSHION IN CLARET VELVET SURROUND

Making surrounds for round cushions is often a problem. This easy method of ruching the velvet in one circular piece can be adapted in many ways, by reducing or increasing the number of ruched panels or pleats. The layout is shown in Fig 11.

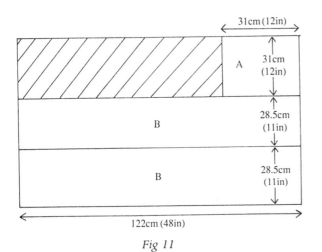

Fig 11

The piece of velvet should be 1m × 115cm (39 × 45in), consisting of:
Back panel 31 × 31cm (12 × 12in) – to produce a circle diameter of 31cm (12in).
Two pieces for ruched surround 28.5 × 122cm (11 × 48in) each.

TO MEASURE AND CUT OUT PANELS
Measure and mark materials into panels with tailor's chalk, to sizes as specified above.

Alternatively, make patterns in paper of above sizes and pin to material, chalking a line around each one. Remove paper patterns and cut out.

TO ASSEMBLE
Take both long panels B and machine stitch them together at both ends, forming a complete circle (see Fig 12).

Fig 12

Now fold the width in half and stitch with a loose tension (to gather later) 4cm (1¹/₂in) from the folded edge (see Fig 13). Sew all the way around and over-sew the first stitches by 4.5cm (1³/₄in), leaving about 15.5cm (6in) of thread to use for pulling up. This is also required at the beginning of your stitches.

Next fold in one of the edges 2cm (³/₄in) and stitch down close to the folded edge. (This is to keep the material from fraying.) See Fig 14 for cross section.

Repeat with the other edge (see Fig 15).

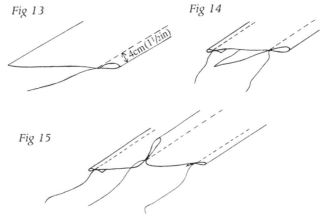

Fig 13 *Fig 14*

Fig 15

Now fold one edge in to meet the centre stitches, this gives another fold which is stitched down ¹/₂cm (¹/₄in) in from the fold, again leaving 16cm (6in) of thread loose, for pulling up later. Repeat on the other side. See Fig 16, which shows a cross section of your material.

Fig 16

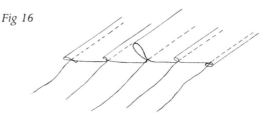

There should now be five lines of stitches ready for gathering with ten lengths of thread (see Fig 17).

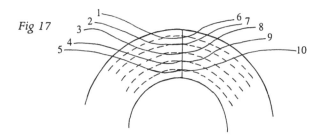

Fig 17

Start gathering by carefully pulling your threads for the centre pleat only. Do this by pulling each of the two threads alternately, evenly gathering up the velvet by moving it along the thread with your fingers until you have a circumference of 152.5cm (60in). Finish off by securing the ends and back stitching several times by hand.

Now pull up one of the small ruched pleats which flank either side of the main centre, gathering until the circumference measures 132.5cm (52in). Repeat this on the other side, securing the ends as before.

There are now two edges left to be gathered. Pull up the gathering on one edge to 102cm (40in).

The circular back panel is now placed in position, by inserting its edge under the edge of the ruching piece by 2cm (¾in). Tack together and machine over the gathered stitches on the outside (see Fig 18).

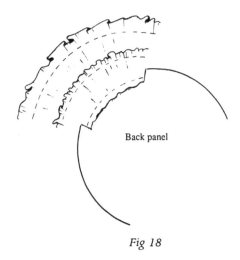

Back panel

Fig 18

Lastly, gather the edge which will be stitched to your tapestry. Check the size by inserting your tapestry. Make sure your work has been correctly pressed (see page 15).

Place your feather cushion or filling inside the velvet surround, then blind hem the velvet to the tapestry.

ADDITIONAL CUTTING LAYOUTS

Method of assembly is the same as for the Autumn Pair of Cushions (see pages 39–41).

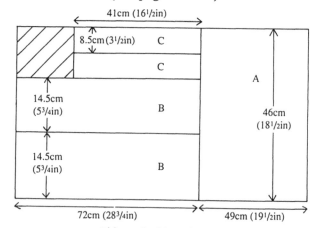

Oblong Cushions (page 79)

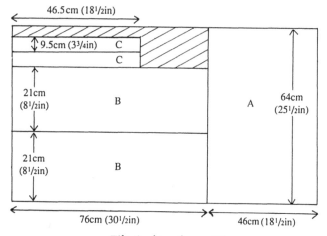

Tile Cushion (page 82)

Method of assembly is the same as for the Small Round Cushion (see pages 41–2).

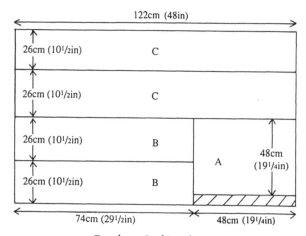

Foxglove Cushion (page 86)

REPEATING PATTERNS

Repeating patterns are extremely useful for many items such as foot and piano stools, chair and bench seats, cushions and so on, where finding a suitably sized design for the item to be covered can sometimes be difficult. You might find that a design almost fits, but that there is a wide area around the design left empty, which can only be filled in with the background colour.

Look at the examples of students' work on this page. The repeating patterns in these designs and the one on page 46 were worked in crewel wool – one strand only – on 14 to the inch double-stranded canvas. They were used for some small round Victorian foot stools which required a small stitch.

Chair seats in particular can be very oddly shaped, and a repeating pattern is obviously the best design to use in this situation. Keep repeating the pattern, copying the design exactly, until the whole area is covered. Try to choose designs that suit the item. For example, a large cushion or chair seat can take a large pattern, and can be worked on larger count canvas such as nine or ten count. For more delicate items, such as foot stools and small cushions, you could use a fourteen-count canvas and sew in fine crewel wool.

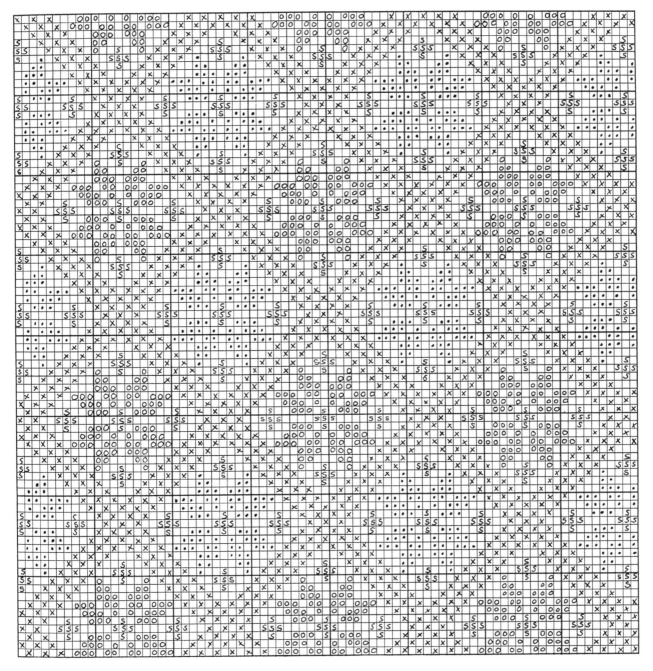

SMALL REPEATING PATTERN IN CREWEL WOOL: 1

FINISHED SIZE: 17 × 14cm (6½ × 5½in)
CANVAS: Fourteen-count, double-stranded
NEEDLE: Size 22 Tapestry

	APPLETON CREWEL WOOL NO/COLOUR	SKEINS
□	715 Dk Mulberry (Background)	4
/	711 Pale Lilac	1
O	753 Med Pink	1
•	752 Pale Pink	1
X	334 Green	1

SMALL REPEATING PATTERN IN CREWEL WOOL: 2

FINISHED SIZE: 17 × 14cm (6½ × 5½in)
CANVAS: Fourteen-count, double-stranded
NEEDLE: Size 22 Tapestry

	APPLETON CREWEL WOOL NO/COLOUR	SKEINS
□	332 Lt Green (Background)	4
•	713 Mauve	1
S	934 Dk Mauve	1
O	145 Pink	1
X	337 Dk Green	1

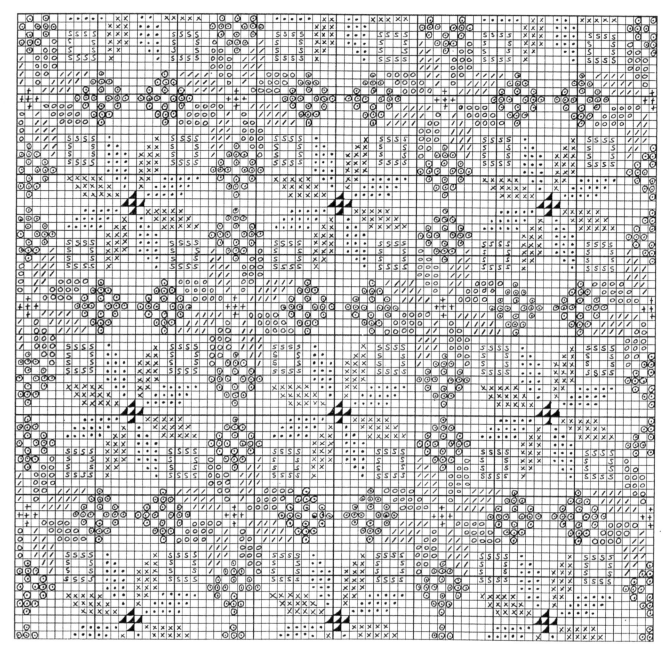

REPEATING PATTERN: 1

FINISHED SIZE: 28 × 23cm (11 × 9in)
CANVAS: 38 × 33cm (15 × 13in) nine-count, double-stranded
NEEDLE: Size 20 Tapestry

	APPLETON TAPESTRY WOOL NO/COLOUR	SKEINS (HANKS)
☐	585 Dk Brown (Background)	15 (2½)
+	477 Bright Orange	2
	471 Lt Yellow	1
S	313 Lt Green	3
/	765 Lt Tan	5
O	697 Dk Tan	5
•	695 Lt Gold	4
X	696 Dk Gold	4
O	315 Dk Green	5

REPEATING PATTERN: 2

FINISHED SIZE: 28 × 23cm (11 × 9in)
CANVAS: Nine-count, double-stranded
NEEDLE: Size 20 Tapestry

	APPLETON TAPESTRY WOOL NO/COLOUR	SKEINS (HANKS)
☐	202 Pinky Beige (Background)	12 (2)
X	758 Dk Red	2
O	754 Med Pink	4
•	941 Pale Pink	3
S	157 Dk Green	3
/	644 Lt Green	3

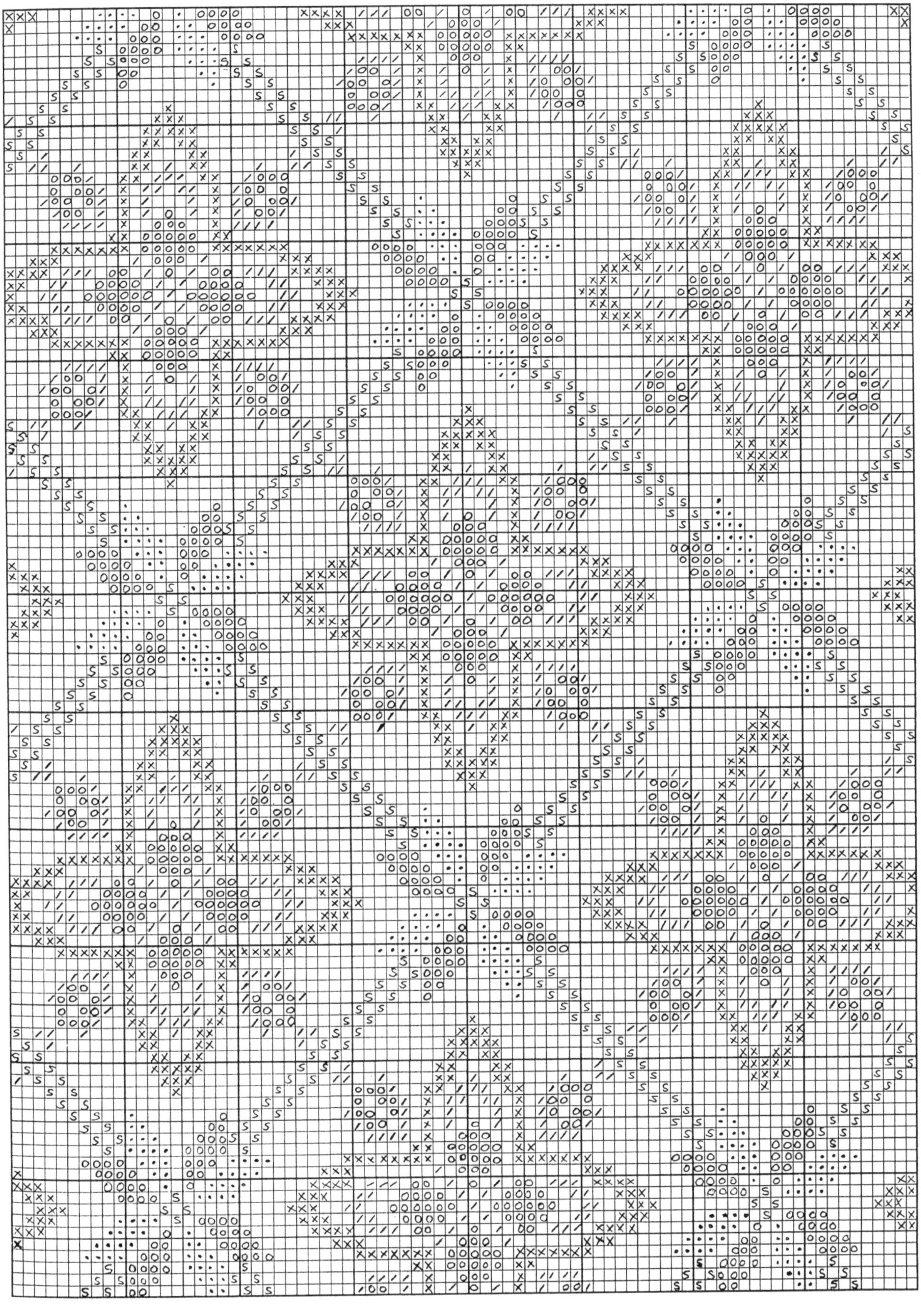

REPEATING PATTERN: 3

FINISHED SIZE: 28 × 23cm (11 × 9in)
CANVAS: Nine-count, double-stranded
NEEDLE: Size 20 Tapestry

	APPLETON TAPESTRY WOOL NO/COLOUR	SKEINS (HANKS)
□	585 Dk Brown (Background)	9 (1½)
O	581 Custard Yellow	2
X	186 Beige	6 (1)
S	244 Green	6 (1)
/	912 Faun	4
•	763 Lt Brown	4

COMPLETE DESIGNS FOR CUSHIONS AND WALLHANGINGS

ICELANDIC STAR

Many students refer to this design as the 'snow-flake'. Stitched in four delicious shades of blue, it is relatively easy to work as the petal shapes can be sewn individually. The design can be made up into either a cushion or a framed picture.

There are many other star designs to be found in Icelandic embroidery, large patterns being used in cushions and smaller ones incorporated in a variety of borders.

ICELANDIC KNOT

This design was adapted from part of a traditional Icelandic woven bed coverlet. I actually took an Appleton colour swatch to the National Museum in Iceland and matched the colours, as near as possible, to the original.

It is the easiest to stitch of all the designs in this book – perfect for the beginner. It is also suitable for young children to work, being very easy to count out. The dramatic black background contrasts well with the brightness of the other nine colours.

TOP

ICELANDIC STAR

FINISHED SIZE: 31 × 31cm (12 × 12in)
CANVAS: 46 × 46cm (18 × 18in) nine-count, double-stranded
NEEDLE: Size 20 Tapestry

	APPLETON TAPESTRY WOOL NO/COLOUR	SKEINS (HANKS)
□	461 Pale Blue (Background)	9 (1½)
O	748 Navy Blue	6 (1)
+	463 Lt Cornflower Blue	2
‖	464 Dk Cornflower Blue	6 (1)

ICELANDIC KNOT

FINISHED SIZE: 18 × 18cm (7 × 7in)
CANVAS: 31 × 31cm (12 × 12in) nine-count, double-stranded
NEEDLE: Size 20 Tapestry

	APPLETON TAPESTRY WOOL NO/COLOUR	SKEINS
□	993 Black (Background)	4
•	991 White	1
S	552 Bright Yellow	1
O	471 Pale Yellow	1
■	946 Bright Pink	1
X	747 Dk Blue	1
\	562 Lt Blue	1
‖	144 Pale Mauve	2
—	564 Med Blue	2
+	482 Turquoise	1

LARGE ICELANDIC KNOT

The large Icelandic knot design is a detail from a multi-coloured woven bed coverlet from the latter part of the eighteenth century (shown right). The Celtic style of interlocking shapes is emphasised if the background colour is left in the apertures, as shown in the tapestry with a black background. Compare the example shown inset right, which has coloured stitches sewn into the apertures – the former seems to work better. The acorn design was a symbol used in embroidery to depict strength.

The chart has been extended to make it easier to see how the repeating pattern is formed. It also incorporates a star pattern not shown in the stitched example.

LARGE ICELANDIC KNOT

FINISHED SIZE: 35 × 42cm (14 × 16½in)
CANVAS: 45 × 52cm (18 × 20½in)
nine-count, double-stranded
NEEDLE: Size 20 Tapestry

	APPLETON TAPESTRY WOOL NO/COLOUR		SKEINS (HANKS)
☐	993	Black (Background)	24 (4)
O	823	Dk Blue	3
X	821	Lt Blue	3
/	991	White	4
V	313	Gold	2
S	144	Pink	4
◢	148	Dk Pink	4
II	351	Lt Green	1
•	703	Pinky Beige	4

ALTERNATIVE COLOURWAYS

	APPLETON TAPESTRY WOOL NO/COLOUR		SKEINS (HANKS)
☐	992	Off White (Background)	26 (4½)
◢	505	Dk Red	6
S	503	Lt Red	6
O	747	Dk Blue	6
X	744	Lt Blue	6
•V	552	Yellow	6
V•	553	Turquoise Green	3
II			

Where two symbols are shown for one colour, please refer to the colour photograph

FLOWERS AND VASE

One of the first designs I produced, and perhaps one of the most popular, is the Icelandic Flowers and Vase pattern, a small geometric stylised vase of flowers, sewn in lilacs, pinks and greens.

A great deal of Icelandic embroidery was sewn on dark woven cloth using bright colours for the design, which produced a dramatic contrast. The same applies when sewing in dark, rich colours onto a light, natural-coloured background. It does not matter whether the filling in is dark or light so long as the contrast is there.

Some people might find the damson colour used in this design difficult to see. It helps to sew this area during the lightest hours of the day, sitting by a window, rather than struggling with it by electric light in the evening.

LARGE VASE OF FLOWERS

This large vase of flowers was first chosen and adapted for a magazine readers' offer. One of my students, Hilda Lester, had originally stitched it using brighter colours which contrasted with a black background, and this inspired me to design something similar.

Being geometric, it is easy to follow. Start stitching from the centre stem and gradually balance out the design either side of the stem – remember that counting your spaces is as important as counting your stitches. Hilda, although elderly, coped well with the black background.

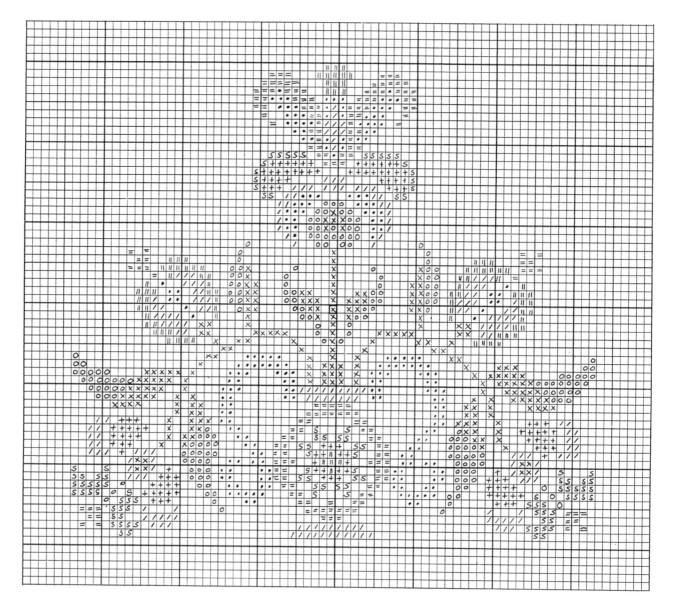

FLOWERS AND VASE

FINISHED SIZE: 20 × 18cm (8 × 7in)
CANVAS: 33 × 30cm (13 × 12in) nine-count, double-stranded
NEEDLE: Size 20 Tapestry

	APPLETON TAPESTRY WOOL NO/COLOUR	SKEINS (HANKS)
□	106 Damson (Background)	8 (1¼)
O	342 Lt Green	1
X	345 Dk Green	1
‖	451 Lt Mauve	1
/	453 Med Mauve	1
•	455 Dk Mauve	1
S	711 Lt Pink	1
+	144 Med Pink	1
=	801 Bright Cerise	1

LARGE VASE OF FLOWERS

FINISHED SIZE: 36 × 30cm (14 × 12in)
CANVAS: 51 × 46cm (20 × 18in) nine-count, double-stranded
NEEDLE: Size 20 Tapestry

	APPLETON TAPESTRY WOOL NO/COLOUR	SKEINS (HANKS)
□	106 Damson (Background)	21 (3)
S	801 Lt Cerise	2
/	802 Med Cerise	1
O	805 Dk Cerise	3
G	333 Lt Green	1
Λ	334 Med Green	2
+	336 Dk Green	1
X	604 Lt Lilac	2
•	105 Dk Lilac	3
θ	711 Dusky Pink	2
V	941 Baby Pink	1
=	716 Dk Maroon	2

BORDERED VASE WITH FLOWERS

This is a typical example of a central design with border surround, as explained on pages 28 and 29. On this occasion, two similar borders have been used. Top and bottom there is a rope pattern with flowers, while the side borders have a zigzag line with more flowers.

In the rope pattern the apertures were left open and filled with the background colour. This was not always done on original works but, as in the

Icelandic Knot pattern (see page 58), it gives a three-dimensional feeling.

The Icelandic design and borders were adapted, the colours chosen and the prototype tapestry stitched – all in one weekend. It has become even more popular than the Flowers and Vase pattern shown on page 62. Perhaps the subtle shades of antique mauves and pinks blend more easily into today's interior colour schemes.

BIRDS AND DRAGONS

This design was adapted from sections of a bed coverlet dated 1811, now housed in the National Museum, Reykjavik. The original tapestry was sewn in long-armed cross stitch and small amounts of Florentine stitch.

The colourways shown here were chosen by two of my students, and not in traditional shades. Whichever colours you choose, this design is equally effective worked as a wallhanging or as a cushion.

BORDERED VASE WITH FLOWERS

FINISHED SIZE: 30 × 27cm (12 × 10½in)
CANVAS: 38 × 38cm (15 × 15in)
nine-count, double-stranded
NEEDLE: Size 20 Tapestry

	APPLETON TAPESTRY WOOL NO/COLOUR	SKEINS (HANKS)		APPLETON TAPESTRY WOOL NO/COLOUR	SKEINS
□	121 Pinky Beige (Centre Background)	7 (1)	•	752 Pale Pink	1
□	931 Dull Mauve (Border Background)	7 (1)	O	153 Lt Green	2
			II	158 Dk Green	4
S	755 Rose Pink	3	+	715 Claret	3
			/	935 Dk Claret	3

BIRDS AND DRAGONS

FINISHED SIZE: 44 × 44cm (17 × 17in)
CANVAS: 54 × 54cm (21 × 21in) nine-count, double-stranded
NEEDLE: Size 20 Tapestry

	APPLETON TAPESTRY WOOL NO/COLOUR	SKEINS (HANKS)
□	762 Pinky Beige (Background)	18 (3)
•	991 White	2
O	208 Red	3
S	524 Lt Turquoise	2
X	526 Dk Turquoise	6

<u>ALTERNATIVE COLOURWAY</u>

	APPLETON TAPESTRY WOOL NO/COLOUR	SKEINS (HANKS)
□	296 Dk Green (Background)	12 (2)
X	293 Lt Green	9
◢	121 Pinky Beige	2
O	207 Russet	2
•	694 Yellow	1
V	991 White	1

PINK OBLONG CUSHION

This cushion in salmony pinks is one half of the blue saddle cloth design (see page 91).

While watching a television chat show, my eye was caught by a salmon-coloured cushion on the arm of a chair. Grabbing my camera, I managed to get a good photograph and the developed print enabled me to match the pale salmony colours.

OBLONG PINK CUSHION

FINISHED SIZE: 53 × 36cm (20½ × 14in)
CANVAS: 63 × 47cm (24½ × 18in)
nine-count, double-stranded
NEEDLE: Size 20 Tapestry

	APPLETON TAPESTRY WOOL NO/COLOUR	SKEINS
■	935 Plum Brown (Background)	26
S	203 Pinky Beige	2
X	222 Deep Rose Pink	5
=	350 Pale Green	3
O	705 Palest Peach	3
/	223 Med Rose Pink	6
•	992 White	1
C	621 Peach	1
W	962 Pale Blue	1

| | 935 | **S** | 203 | **X** | 222 | **=** | 350 | **O** | 705 | **/** | 223 | **•** | 992 | **C** | 621 | **W** | 962 |

AUTUMN PAIR
OF CUSHIONS

This pair of gold, russet and green cushions have an autumnal feel about them. Both cushions use the same range of colours, although two more shades are used in the same design on this page. The rich gold and orange colours contrast beautifully with the dark green background.

The crisp, bold designs are easy to sew and make up a medium-sized cushion of 28 × 28cm (11 × 11in). For instructions on how to make the ruched velvet surround shown here (exactly the same on each cushion) see pages 39–41.

AUTUMN CUSHION: 1

FINISHED SIZE: 28 × 28cm (11 × 11in)
CANVAS: 38 × 38cm (15 × 15in) nine-count, double-stranded
NEEDLE: Size 20 Tapestry

	APPLETON TAPESTRY WOOL NO/COLOUR	SKEINS			APPLETON TAPESTRY WOOL NO/COLOUR	SKEINS
□	158 Dk Turquoise	11 (2)		I	478 Dk Orange	4
•	691 Beige	2		◢	184 Lt Brown	1
X	644 Lt Turquoise	3		S	187 Dk Brown	3
O	475 Lt Orange	2		/	473 Yellow	2

AUTUMN CUSHION: 2

Finished Size: 28 × 28cm (11 × 11in)
Canvas: 38 × 38cm (15 × 15in) nine-count, double-stranded
Needle: Size 20 Tapestry

	APPLETON TAPESTRY WOOL NO/COLOUR	SKEINS (HANKS)		APPLETON TAPESTRY WOOL NO/COLOUR	SKEINS
☐	158 Dk Turquoise (Background)	11 (2)	**O**	475 Lt Orange	4
•	691 Beige	2	**I**	478 Dk Orange	3
X	644 Lt Turquoise	4	**S**	187 Dk Brown	1

77

GRANDMOTHER'S CUSHION

This is one of my favourite cushions from Grand-mother Hanna. The colour combination, although rich, is subtle. The cross-stitched design is worked on a type of tabby or floba cloth (available from the Icelandic Tapestry School) which is left showing as the background. So instead of a background filled in with cross stitch as in canvas work, the cloth itself becomes the background, its colour lending a neutral tone to the colourful design. You could, of course, stitch the design on canvas and fill in the background. The design also incorporates dramatic sections in black.

Hanna had a natural gift for combining colours – a gift my mother insists I have inherited. Certainly I never have any problem choosing colour combinations – if a student asks my advice about a colour for their background, I can make my choice imme-diately.

OBLONG CUSHIONS

The oblong cushions are shown in two very differ-ent colourways. This came about because of a request for a new cushion design. When finished it was thought to be far too pale – my attempt to create an antique-looking colour scheme did not suit the customer!

A second cushion was stitched in the same pattern, but this time with strong vibrant colours in greens, cerise and pinks, finishing with a dramatic contrasting background of damson.

This combination was not acceptable either, and the pursuit of the elusive suitable colour scheme was eventually shelved. However, the designs have been included in this book because many students have admired the colour combinations and have asked for copies of the design and the wools.

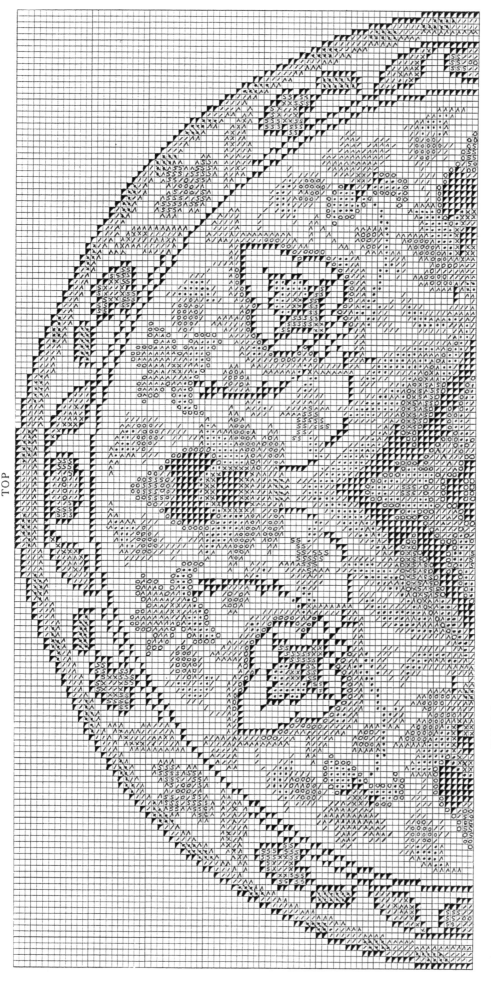

TOP

GRANDMOTHER'S CUSHION

Finished Size: 45cm (17½in) diam
Canvas: 58 × 58cm (23 × 23in)
Floba cloth
Needle: Size 22 Tapestry

	PATERNA WOOL NO/COLOUR		SKEIN
\	D211	Red	5
O	454	Beige	5
X	727	Yellow	2
•	D516	Dk Green	3
⚹	D556	Lt Turquoise Green	2
S	564	Pale Blue	2
>	431	Dk Brown	5
◣	220	Black	5

Use one strand only of the 3-strand wool
throughout

OBLONG CUSHION

Finished Size: 46 × 31cm (18 × 12in)
Canvas: 56 × 41cm (22 × 16in)
nine-count, double-stranded
Needle: Size 20 Tapestry

	APPLETON TAPESTRY WOOL NO/COLOUR		SKEIN (HANK
☐	106	Damson (Background)	19 (3½
V	525	Lt Turquoise	2
–	528	Dk Turquoise	3
‖	942	Lt Rose	1
S	945	Med Rose	1
O	947	Dk Rose	2
G	451	Lt Mauve	1
◣	454	Dk Mauve	3
•	801	Lt Fuchsia	2
X	805	Dk Fuchsia	3

LILAC COLOURWAY

There is no separate chart for this colourway
You will need to check the colour photograp
for the positioning of some shades: there ar
two extra colours in this version

☐	972	Greeny Grey (Background)	18 (3)
	103	Dk Purple	1
	101	Lt Purple	1
	105	Dk Lilac	1
	603	Med Lilac	1
	601	Pinky Lilac	1
	607	Dk Mauve	4
	604	Lt Mauve	1
	106	Navy	4
	716	Deep Maroon	4
	713	Deep Pink	2
	753	Med Pink	1
	752	Baby Pink	1

TOP

TILE CUSHION

Reminiscent of a ceramic tile, this design is sewn in a typical Icelandic colour scheme reminding one of natural dyes.

This is not a design for a beginner, as the stitch counting in the corners is tricky. Although geometric, the corner designs with the gold flowers are fairly complicated, and peace and quiet and a clear head are essential for accurate counting. But the results are worth it!

For instructions for making up the ruched velvet surround see page 42. The cushion is shown made up on page 87. (If you are wondering about the significance of the dried sunflower head, there isn't any, it was just nice to include it in the photograph. It is one of my favourite flowers and it is fascinating to think that one seed can produce such a giant plant in such a short spell of summer days.)

ROUND CUSHION

The observant eye will note that this design is slightly similar to my grandmother's large cushion shown on page 78. In fact, I have adapted part of that design to make a smaller cushion of 28cm (11in) diameter, extending to 48cm (19in) diameter when the velvet surround is added.

The combination of soft lilac, pink and green colours fits into the decor of most homes. To make the ruched velvet surround, see pages 41–2.

TOP

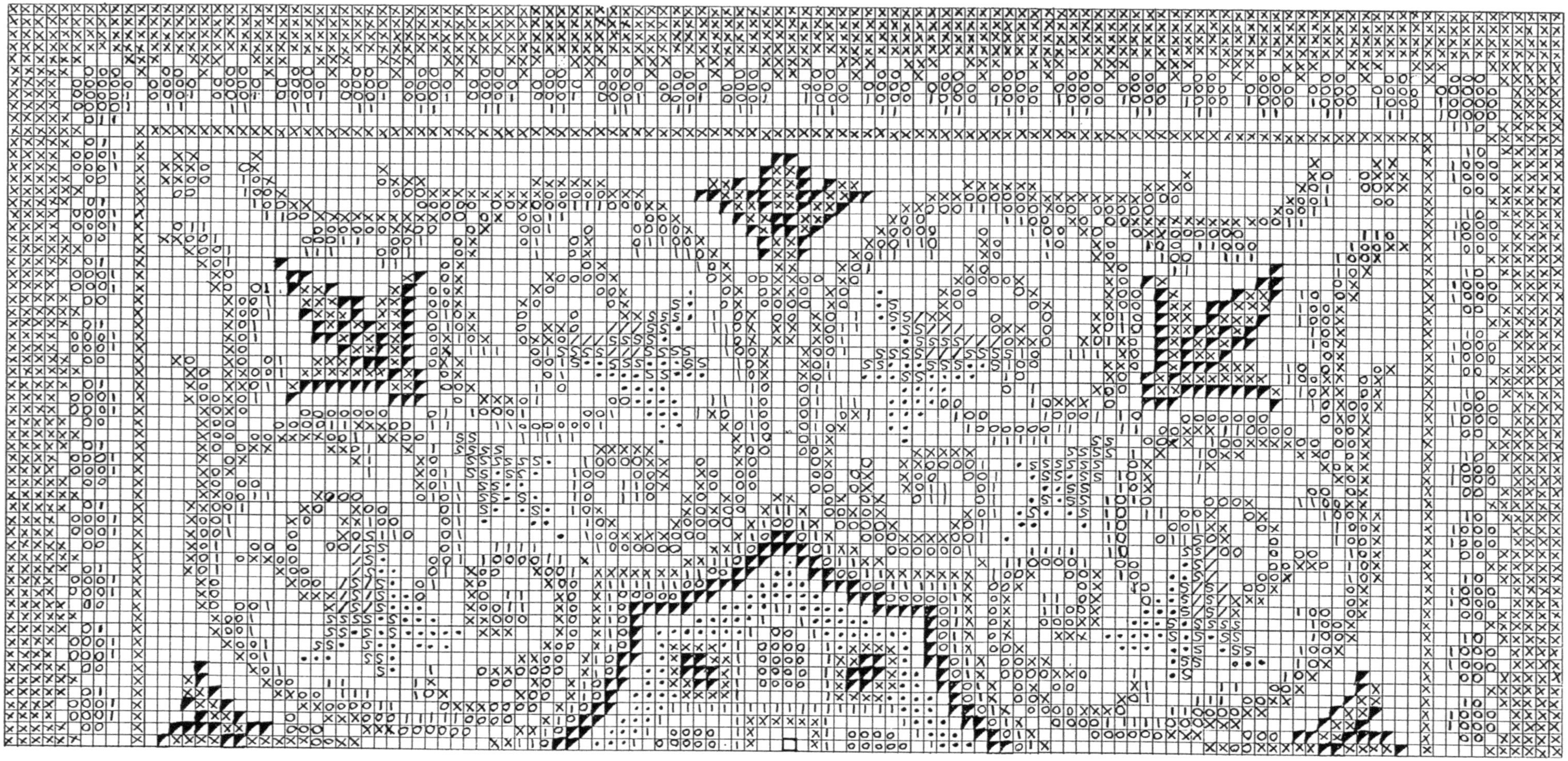

TILE CUSHION

Finished Size: 36 × 36cm (14 × 14in)
Canvas: 46 × 46cm (18 × 18in) nine-count, double-stranded
Needle: Size 20 Tapestry

	APPLETON TAPESTRY WOOL NO/COLOUR	SKEINS (HANKS)
□	987 Beige (Background)	11 (2)
O	245 Dk Green	6 (1)
I	243 Lt Green	4
/	316 Dk Yellow Green	1
S	314 Med Yellow Green	3
•	311 Lt Yellow Green	3
X	585 Dk Brown	8 (1½)
◤	227 Dk Red	4

ROUND CUSHION

Finished Size: 28cm (11in) diameter
Canvas: 38 × 38cm (15 × 15in) nine-count, double-stranded
Needle: Size 20 Tapestry

	APPLETON TAPESTRY WOOL NO/COLOUR	SKEINS (HANKS)
□	181 Beige (Background)	12 (2)
O	298 Dk Green	2
I	293 Lt Green	2
S	716 Dk Wine	4
•	223 Pink	3
X	712 Pale Lilac	3
◤	693 Yellow	1

FOXGLOVE CUSHION

The foxglove cushion is perhaps the only design that is not geometric nor stylised in its flowered design. Until recently we were not sure whether Grandmother Hanna had created the design, or whether it had originated from another source. A student has written to say that she thinks the design comes from Norway. Wherever it came from, it certainly is a very pretty picture of foxgloves.

Grandmother's original had about forty colours in it. This has been whittled down to twenty-three, which still produces a very colourful tapestry.

The colours are easy to sort out; all the flowers have four shades of each colour in the pink, mauve and cream. Likewise, the two different colours of green leaves have four shades each.

Start by stitching the centre pink flower marked on the chart. Then stitch its neighbour on either side, gradually extending out, top to bottom, and side to side, sewing one flower at a time.

This is a substantial cushion, finishing with a canvas diameter of 50cm (19½in). Velvet surround cut out sizes are on page 42.

FOXGLOVE CUSHION

FINISHED SIZE: 50 × 50cm (19½ × 19½in)
CANVAS: 61 × 61cm (24 × 24in) nine-count,
double-stranded
NEEDLE: Size 20 Tapestry

		APPLETON TAPESTRY WOOL NO/COLOUR	SKEINS (HANKS)
□		181 Soft Pinky Beige (Background)	14 (2½)

PINK FLOWERS

⚡		227 Deep Red	2
S		224 Med Pink	3
\\		222 Dusty Pink	2
/		752 Palest Pink	2

MAUVE FLOWERS

↗		935 Darkest Mauve	1
✖		714 Deep Pinky Mauve	1
‖		712 Med Mauve	2
⊙		142 Lt Pinky Mauve	2

BEIGE FLOWERS

•		992 Off White	2
⊃		984 Lt Beige	2
⚡		953 Med Beige	1
▲		955 Dk Beige	1

GOLD LEAVES

Y		311 Golden Brown	1
0		313 Med Golden Brown	2
●		315 Dk Golden Brown	3
↖		298 Darkest Green	3

GREEN LEAVES

⋊		641 Palest Green	2
⅔		643 Med Green	2
X		645 Dk Green	2
↖		298 Darkest Green	*

STEMS

↘		345 Mid Olive Green	3
V		348 Dk Olive Green	1

FLOWER CENTRES

<		471 Yellow	1

* Quantity included above under Gold Leaves

THE BLUE TAPESTRY

In Iceland in the early days ladies rode side-saddle on sturdy horses, descendants of the original breed brought over by the early Norse settlers. To protect their costumes, beautifully decorated horse cloths were either woven or embroidered.

The beginning of my fascination with Icelandic embroidery lay in one of my mother's books, called *Ancient Icelandic Art*. I was struck by the beautiful pattern of a horse cloth. (An interesting point to note is that the design of flowers at the top of the pattern became upright once thrown over the horse's flank.) Some of you may recall the days when most books only had a few coloured photographs, the majority being only in black and white, which was my problem in this case. The photograph of the saddle cloth was in shades of black and white and this was the only indication of colour change. So, blue being my favourite colour, I chose eleven shades of blue.

When my work was nearly finished I took it on holiday with me to Iceland, and went to the National Museum in Reykjavik to compare it with the original. Imagine my surprise at finding it ten times the size of mine, sewn in a completely different stitch to my cross stitch and multi-coloured!

The ladies working in the museum complimented me on my achievement, although it was very different from the beautiful original.

The end result can be seen here with the chart on the following pages. It is also available as a kit from the Icelandic Tapestry School.

There are many beautiful examples of these cloths on display in the National Museum of Iceland in Reykjavik. Don't miss the ones in the basement.

90

THE BLUE TAPESTRY

FINISHED SIZE: 50 × 63cm
(19½ × 25in)
CANVAS: 61 × 76cm (24 × 30in)
nine-count, double-stranded
NEEDLE: Size 20 Tapestry

	APPLETON TAPESTRY WOOL NO/COLOUR	SKEINS (HANKS)
☐	748 Dk Blue (Background)	36 (6)
•	992 Snow White	8 (1⅓)
X	886 Glacier Blue	4
‖	921 Silver Birch	5
O	742 Geysir Blue	5
<	822 Fjörd Blue	2
S	821 Sky Blue	3
+	922 Lichen Grey	2
O	744 Waterfall Blue	2
/	324 Lava Blue	6 (1)

Tapestry by Pamela Drummond. The two main designs are charted on pages 97 and 100.

ICELANDIC BED COVERLETS

Traditional Icelandic bed coverlets – essential household items in such a climate – were made using either woollen or linen tabby, upon which the original 'cross stitch' was sewn. This was a treble cross stitch, completed as one worked along the row. Originally called cross stitch, it now has to be differentiated from modern cross stitch by calling it *long-armed*, long-legged, treble or *braid* stitch. This stitch produced a warm and hard-wearing article, and examples date back to the medieval period.

My favourite, and perhaps the most famous of all Icelandic coverlets executed entirely in long-armed stitch, is the Coverlet of the Knights, known in Iceland as the *Riddarateppid* (see photograph on page 110). It is housed in the National Museum, Reykjavik.

The popular colour combinations of red, blue, green and white with a yellow background were often used. The examples of my students' work on pages 106–7 and 111 show the typical designs and combination of colours.

Later, in the seventeenth century 'eye stitch' was introduced and worked in small areas, linking together larger pictorial sections worked in long-armed stitch. The eye stitch was also used decoratively in the borders, enhancing the work still further. Working these two stitches together on one piece is very distinctive and might be unique to Icelandic embroidery.

The religious theme of the bed coverlet using both these stitches (page 10) shows the four stages of the life of Christ. Each picture is encircled by a leaf and stem border, the two half circles at the bottom showing part of the Tree of Life and Noah's Ark. It is thought this was especially designed for an Icelandic bishop. Scenes from the Bible were often depicted in embroidery pieces.

The National Museum of Iceland houses another bed coverlet completely sewn in eye stitch – quite a feat, when you consider the meticulous counting of threads on the material necessary to achieve the perfect geometric design and the sixteen individual stitches that have to be sewn to create each eye stitch.

Recently, while working on an eye stitch design, my counting went adrift, and I had to face the laborious task of unpicking. A total of 20 eye stitches were incorrect, meaning 320 individual stitches had to be unpicked! It will certainly teach me to count correctly in the future, and also to remember to consider my *spaces* as important as my stitches.

The designs shown on the pages which follow have been inspired by and adapted from traditional coverlets, many from the Coverlet of the Knights itself. Individual designs can be stitched as charted, or can be combined with each other and surrounded by borders to create spectacular large wall hangings.

KNIGHT ON HORSEBACK WITH HOUND AND FALCON

This chart represents the design of a hunter or knight depicted in the circular frame on the right-hand side of the tapestry shown on pages 94–5. The points of the four red triangles top, bottom and sides are shown by the heavy circular symbols, and the inner edge of the blue circular frame is partly charted as a guide to this design, which is charted in full on page 101.

Although red, blue, green and white with a yellow background were traditionally used for these coverlets, there is absolutely no reason why you cannot use completely different colours from the ones shown.

KNIGHT ON HORSEBACK
WITH HOUND AND FALCON

FINISHED SIZE: 38 × 38cm (15 × 15in)
CANVAS: 51 × 51cm (20 × 20in) nine-count, double-stranded
NEEDLE: Size 20 Tapestry

Quantities given include blue circle and corner designs, as page 101

	APPLETON TAPESTRY WOOL NO/COLOUR		SKEINS (HANKS)
☐	694	Yellow (Background)	30 (5)
O	504	Red	9 (1½)
/	835	Green	6 (1)
X	747	Blue	15 (2½)
•	991	White	6 (1)

97

HUNTER, DOG, STAG AND FALCON

This design represents the hunter or knight depicted in the circular frame on the lefthand side of the large tapestry stitched by one of my students, Pamela Drummond who worked the whole tapestry in treble cross stitch as shown on pages 94–5. Readers work in full cross stitch from the chart, for tapestry above.

Again, the points of the four red triangles top, bottom and sides are shown by the heavy circular symbols, and again, the inner edge of the blue circular frame is partly charted as a guide. See page 101 for chart of complete circular frame.

In this picture a stag is shown being chased by a hound. The horse looks rather strange and would perhaps feature better as a character in the *Magic Roundabout*, but this only adds charm to these historical designs.

MYTHICAL BEASTIES

Many mythical beasties are depicted in Icelandic embroideries, and the two dragons facing each other are typical. A combination of borders and corners has been added around the circular motif to enlarge the tapestry. Similar beasties are to be found on page 115. Many of the designs date back to the medieval period.

The two dragons are sewn first, gradually work-ing out to the circular frame. The flower and stem design within the blue circular frame is stitched in white, and the background of the four squares, top, bottom and sides is also sewn in white. Once the circular frame is complete the background of the centre can be filled in before stitching the corner designs. This method can also be applied to the charts on pages 108 and 109.

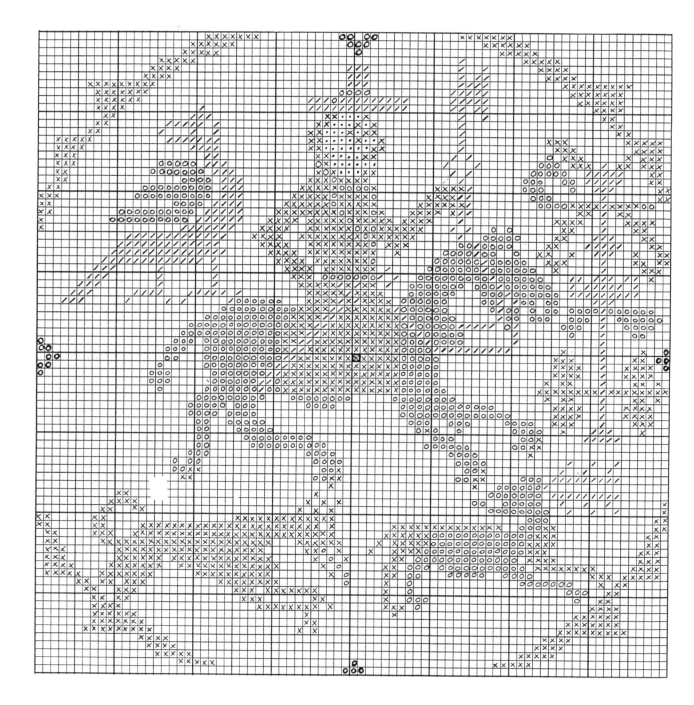

HUNTER, DOG, STAG AND FALCON

FINISHED SIZE: 38 × 38cm (15 × 15in)
CANVAS: 51 × 51cm (20 × 20in) nine-count, double-stranded
NEEDLE: Size 20 Tapestry

	APPLETON TAPESTRY WOOL NO/COLOUR	SKEINS (HANKS)
☐	694 Yellow (Background)	30 (5)
O	504 Red	9 (1½)
/	835 Green	6 (1)
X	747 Blue	15 (2½)
•	991 White	6 (1)

Quantities given include corner designs but *not* border

MYTHICAL BEASTIES

FINISHED SIZE: 41 × 41cm (16 × 16in)
CANVAS: 56 × 56cm (22 × 22in) nine-count, double-stranded
NEEDLE: Size 20 Tapestry

	APPLETON TAPESTRY WOOL NO/COLOUR	SKEINS (HANKS)
☐	694 Yellow (Background)	30 (5)
O	504 Red	9 (1½)
X	465 Blue	15 (2½)
●	833 Green	6 (1)
•	991 White	6 (1)

Quantities given include corner designs, but *not* border

KNIGHT ON HORSEBACK

My son, Lawrence, inspired me to create a design of this famous knight on horseback. Having taught my four children cross stitch, at the age of ten Lawrence had become completely hooked. So engrossed was he that he would rise one hour earlier each morning in order to cross stitch before he went to school, and so particular was he, that he would tediously unpick lumpy or uneven stitches and redo them. This attitude is usual with all male students, most producing better work than the ladies – sorry girls! Lawrence's knight on horseback is seen inset left.

BISHOP AT TABLE

Before I discovered nine-count canvas I remember a male student who came to classes bringing pliers and a hammer: the pliers were used to pull the needle through when the going got tough on the ten-count canvas, and the hammer was used vigorously to flatten lumpy stitches!

The Bishop was created to partner the Knight, both being adapted from the famous Coverlet of the Knights, and could be worked together as a pair.

The traditional use of bright red, blue and green with a yellow background is seen here: Appleton colour numbers are given on page 105.

However, because many people would find the colours too bright to fit into their homes, a more subdued combination of the same colours has been introduced: Appleton colour numbers for this version are also given on page 105.

KNIGHT ON HORSEBACK

Finished Size: 31 × 31cm (12 × 12in)
Canvas: 46 × 46cm (18 × 18in) nine-count, double-stranded
Needle: Size 20 Tapestry

	APPLETON TAPESTRY WOOL NO/COLOUR			SKEINS (HANKS)
	BRIGHT	DARK		
□	693	692	Yellow (Background)	12 (2)
O	504	505	Red	5
X	465	749	Blue	5
/	833	834	Green	4
•	991	992	White	1

104

BISHOP AT TABLE

FINISHED SIZE: 31 × 31cm (12 × 12in)

CANVAS: 46 × 46cm (18 × 18in) nine-count, double-stranded

NEEDLE: Size 20 Tapestry

	APPLETON TAPESTRY WOOL NO/COLOUR			SKEINS (HANKS)
	BRIGHT	DARK		
☐	693	692	Yellow (Background)	12 (2)
O	504	505	Red	5
X	465	749	Blue	4
/	833	834	Green	3
•	991	992	White	1

Tapestry by Sarah Tucker

BISHOP

FINISHED SIZE: 22 × 22cm (8½ × 8½in)
CANVAS: 32 × 32cm (12½ × 12½in) nine-count, double-stranded
NEEDLE: Size 20 Tapestry

	APPLETON TAPESTRY WOOL NO/COLOUR			SKEINS (HANKS)
	BRIGHT	DARK		
□	693	692	Yellow (Background)	12 (2)
O	504	505	Red	5
X	465	749	Blue	4
/	833	834	Green	3
•	991	992	White	1

KNIGHT

FINISHED SIZE: 22 × 22cm (8½ × 8½in)
CANVAS: 32 × 32cm (12½ × 12½in) nine-count, double-stranded
NEEDLE: Size 20 Tapestry

	APPLETON TAPESTRY WOOL NO/COLOUR			SKEINS (HANKS)
	BRIGHT	DARK		
□	693	692	Yellow (Background)	12 (2)
O	504	505	Red	5
X	465	749	Blue	5
/	833	834	Green	4
•	991	992	White	1

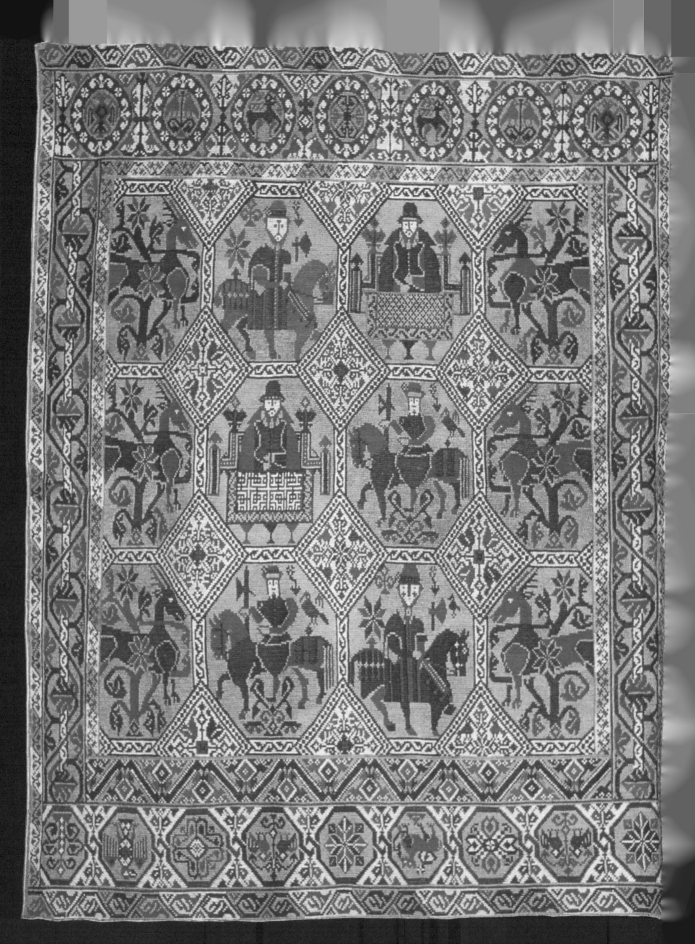

Examples of work by two of my students: Sue Hawkins (above) and Chris Sellars (right)

Left: *The* Riddarateppid *(Coverlet of the Knights) which is housed in the National Museum, Reykjavik (see page 96)*

BORDERS FOR BED COVERLETS

Originals of the borders shown opposite and on pages 116–19 were invariably used for bed coverlets, with many of the designs dating back to medieval times. Sometimes these original coverlets grew from a central theme using famous knights, mythical beasts or ecclesiastical subjects.

A biblical example is the seventeenth-century coverlet, depicting two scenes from the Bible (page 10): Abraham and his son Isaac in the top circle, and in the bottom circle King Herod – who is obviously up to no good! This coverlet is housed in the National Museum in Reykjavik.

My students work in this way, commencing with central panels surrounded by either circular or polygonal frames. As the work progresses the decision is made as to which border is most suitable for the top, bottom and sides. These are then broken up on completion by one row of yellow background, then a row of red followed by another row of yellow. Then more borders are chosen, continuing until a satisfactory size is reached.

A collection of mythical animals surrounded by octagonal frames has been made into a lovely horizontal wall hanging by a student called Pat Lunn, and a selection of fifteen central designs are shown on the following pages.

On a horizontal tapestry such as Pat's, the colours on the knot section of the design should be alternated. The pattern for the top border is inverted at the bottom. Part of the Icelandic knot pattern is stitched in between the octagonal frames as seen completed in the chart on page 118.

The design was traditionally sewn in red and blue or green with a yellow background. The dot symbol can be stitched either in green or blue.

This design is extremely good for beginners to learn on, and is given to students as a counting exercise. The design is first copied onto graph paper, using symbols for the two different colours. One link or shape is drawn at a time, the next shape is then copied close to the one already completed, and so on until the design is finished. The student is made aware that the design has four straight sides, so if a stitch strays from the straight line they immediately know that a mistake has been made.

Having drawn the design, you will find you understand the concept of it much more clearly and make fewer mistakes when stitching.

Start stitching the top shape first. When you have completed it, change your wool colour and go on to the shape closest to it. Use the individual designs as stepping stones. Do not jump to another shape far away – you will invariably miscount. Consider the spaces as important as the stitches.

BORDERS

CANVAS: Nine-count, double-stranded
NEEDLE: Size 20 Tapestry

Quantities of wool given are for length of border shown in the photograph

BORDER 1

	APPLETON NO/COLOUR	SKEINS
O	692 Yellow	4
•	991 White	1
S	505 Red	3
/	835 Green	3
X	749 Blue	3

BORDER 2

	APPLETON NO/COLOUR	SKEINS
O	692 Yellow	4
•	991 White	1
S	505 Red	3
/	835 Green	3
X	749 Blue	3

BORDER 3

	APPLETON NO/COLOUR	SKEINS
−	693 Yellow	2
•	991 White	1
S	504 Red	2
/	834 Green	2
X	465 Blue	2

BORDER 4

	APPLETON NO/COLOUR	SKEINS
−	693 Yellow	2
•	991 White	1
S	504 Red	2
/	834 Green	2
X	465 Blue	2

MEDIEVAL BORDER

CANVAS: Nine-count, double-stranded
NEEDLE: Size 20 Tapestry

	APPLETON TAPESTRY WOOL NO/COLOUR
☐	843 Yellow (Background)
O	697 Rust
S	832 Green
X	824 Blue
•	991 White

Quantities are determined by length of border stitched

116

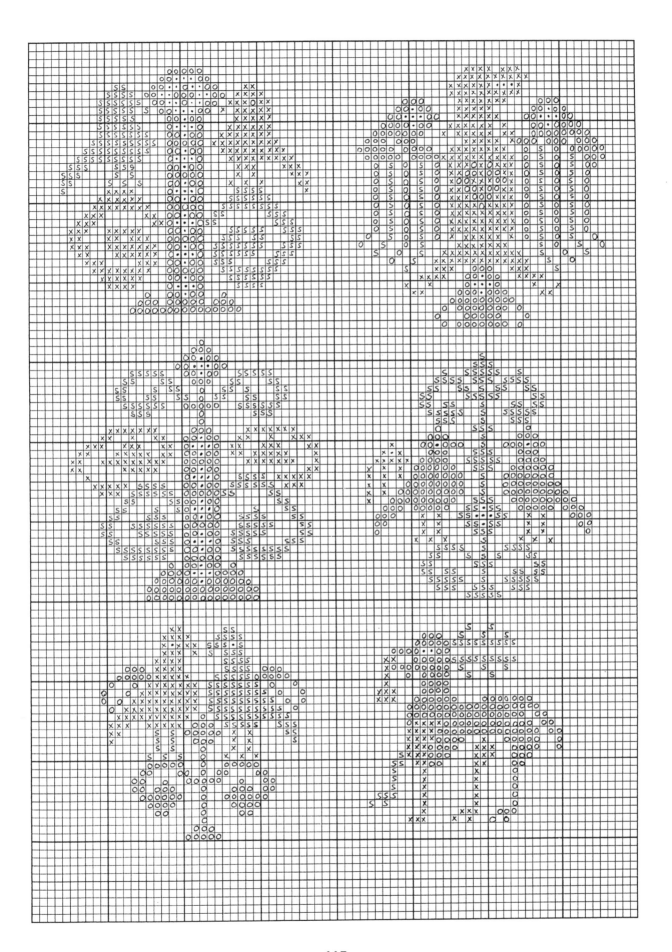

MEDIEVAL BORDER

CANVAS: Nine-count, double-stranded
NEEDLE: Size 20 Tapestry

	APPLETON TAPESTRY WOOL NO/COLOUR
□	843 Yellow (Background)
O	697 Rust
S	832 Green
X	824 Blue
•	991 White

Quantities are determined by length of border stitched

118

MEDIEVAL BORDER

CANVAS: Nine-count, double-stranded
NEEDLE: Size 20 Tapestry

	APPLETON TAPESTRY WOOL NO/COLOUR
□	843 Yellow (Background)
O	697 Rust
S	832 Green
X	824 Blue
•	991 White

Quantities are determined by length of border stitched

119

REINDEER

FINISHED SIZE: 25 × 24cm (10 × 9½in)
CANVAS: 36 × 36cm (14 × 14in) nine-count, double-stranded
NEEDLE: Size 20 Tapestry

	APPLETON TAPESTRY WOOL NO/COLOUR	SKEINS (HANKS)
☐	843 Yellow (Background)	6 (1)
●	504 Red	3
O	825 Blue	3
/	835 Green	3
•	992 Cream	2

GOLDEN DRAGON WITH SNAKES

FINISHED SIZE: 35 × 38cm (14 × 15in)
CANVAS: 46 × 49cm (18 × 19in) nine-count, double-stranded
NEEDLE: Size 20 Tapestry

	APPLETON TAPESTRY WOOL NO/COLOUR	SKEINS (HANKS)
☐	187 Brown (Background)	15 (2½)
☐	696 Dk Autumn Yellow (Background within dragon shape)	5
S	693 Lt Yellow	2
•	694 Med Yellow	3
O	473 Lt Autumn Yellow	2
II	314 Olive Green	1

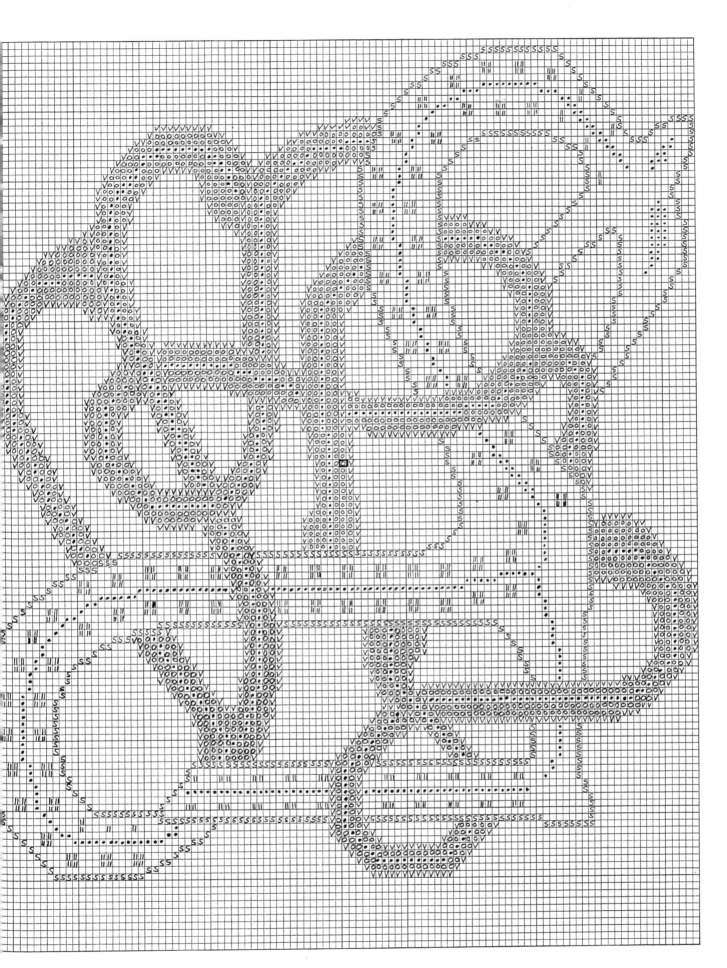

121

REINDEER

The Reindeer, or Icelandic animal pattern, has also
been adapted from the famous Bed Coverlet of the
Knights. On page 110 you can see it in a different
role, used as side panels.

GOLDEN DRAGON
WITH SNAKES

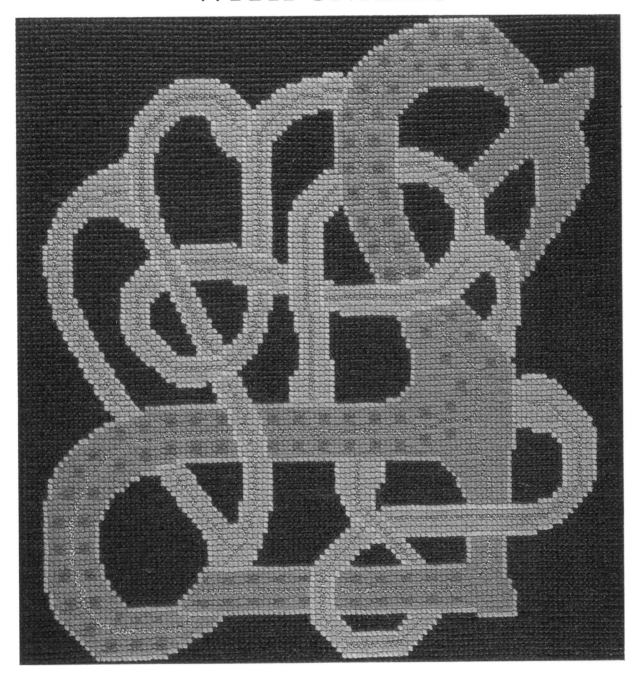

This unique design of a dragon entwined with three snakes in the so-called *Urnes* style is adapted from an eleventh-century brooch found on a lady's costume in a burial mound.

Although the original brooch was worked in silver, and is now available as a replica from the National Museum of Iceland, I have always imagined it would be better worked in gold – hence the choice of golds for this design.

The silver of the original is embossed with small indentations. To imitate this in the tapestry gold thread has been used and worked in cross stitch. Appleton wool colour numbers and the chart are overleaf.

This very striking design has been adopted by the Icelandic Tapestry School as its logo.

ABOUT JÓNA

Since 1985 Jona Sparey has been organising and conducting tours to Iceland, her Mother's homeland

Jóna has been travelling there since she was 6 years old, and therefore knows the country extremely well, also speaking fluent Icelandic.

For first time visitors Jóna organises a special exciting and comprehensive tour brimming over with visits to the North, East and Southern areas of Iceland where many of the most spectacular sites are found.

Visitors return again many times with her to this unique land of contrasts, to other areas such as the North Western Wilderness part of Iceland. The island has a magnetic and magical effect on many.

www.jona-tours.com

ACKNOWLEDGEMENTS

To whom should this book be dedicated?

Should it be my Icelandic grandmother, Hanna, who first taught me the stitches and how to hold the work without the use of a cumbersome frame? (There is no record of a frame ever having been used in Iceland.)

Or should it be to my dear Auntie Nanna – my mother's sister whom I loved so much, while admiring her tremendous talent for sewing in whatever medium?

Or should it be to my mother and her embroidery which inspired me so? Although a tomboy when young, she still managed to embroider beautiful tablecloths and cushions with great perseverance and skill.

Perhaps it should be to Sveinbjörn Thorsteinsson, who introduced me to the National Museum in Reykjavik, where I fell in love with the striking designs and colours of the embroidery exhibited there.

Then again, the ladies of Barnet and Enfield should certainly be mentioned for persuading me to hold classes in embroidery after seeing an exhibition of my work, and the organisers of the Hatfield House Craft Fair, who encouraged me to exhibit there in 1984 when I produced my first four Icelandic tapestry designs.

Perhaps my greatest debt is owed to *all* my students, past and present, for keeping my interest in the subject alive and flourishing through their continuing requests for classes, help and advice.

A mention must also be made of the *Woolcraft* team at Granada Television, who were responsible for my TV debut – a special thank you to Sue Mycock, who instigated the idea of my writing this book.

My very grateful thanks must go to Elsa Gudjónsson, textiles curator of the National Museum of Iceland, who has been most helpful, encouraging me in my interest in Icelandic embroidery and always remembering to update me in all aspects of the art. Her own comprehensive book on the history of Icelandic needlework, *Icelandic Embroidery*, is most popular with my students, and can be obtained from the Icelandic Tapestry School.

Thanks also to Svava, my daughter; Anita, my sister; Erica, my niece; Lara, my daughter; Lawrence, my son; Eve, my neighbour who did all the typing; and stitchers: Pat Acreman, Linda Carter, Margaret Cook, Pamela Drummond, Pat Fraser, Sue Hawkins, Jackie Hopkins, Dot Lucas, Pat Lunn, Angela McGill, Kathleen Medhurst, Sue Openshaw, Sylvia Thomas, Ólina Weightman, Doris White and to all the students who stitched the samples on pages 18–19 and 22–3.

Last, but certainly not least, an acknowledgement should go to my Icelandic ancestors who have instilled in my genes a love of Iceland and its people's rich culture.

Have I forgotten anyone?

PHOTO ACKNOWLEDGEMENTS

The author and publishers would like to thank Philip Jackson for his invaluable contribution to this book in providing the photographs reproduced on pages 27, 30, 31, 34, 35, 46, 47, 50, 51, 54, 55, 62, 63, 66, 70–1, 74, 75, 78, 79, 82, 83, 90–1, 94–5, 102, 103, 106–7, 114, 115, 120, 121 and 126.

All other photographs are by the author.

My mother's home in the centre of Reykjavik was built by her father Jón, and in earlier times looked over the harbour where it was possible to watch the sailing ships out at sea. Jón grew potatoes in a piece of ground in front of the house. It is difficult to imagine this when viewing the same spot today. It is right on the junction of two roads, Bánkerstraeti and Skólavördurstïgur, the hub of city life.

In 1971 the old house was pulled down and replaced by a modern four storey building. This prompted mother's natural Icelandic instinct to write a poem in memory of the old house. In that same year mother celebrated her sixtieth birthday. So, as a tribute to her, her poem, and the house, this tapestry was sewn.

The years go by, and we all become old
But please remember we miss you sorely
You have stood well and long
And given all you had to give.

I remember so well
You needed help to carry on
Your roof needed some repair
Then Venni and I took hands together
To scrape and paint you.

I know you will forgive
If I let fall a few tears
For Mother and Father as well
You were their very life and soul.

Memories of you live on
With Nanna, Venni and me,
Go now in peace, my dear old house
We will never ever forget you.

INDEX

CPSIA information can be obtained
at www.ICGtesting.com
Printed in the USA
LVHW071035121121
703159LV00012B/44